HOW TO START A SUCCESSFUL CREATIVE AGENCY

ESSENTIAL BUSINESS GUIDE

FOR GRAPHIC DESIGNERS, COPYWRITERS, FILMMAKERS, PHOTOGRAPHERS, AND PROGRAMMERS

ANDY STROTE

HOW TO START A SUCCESSFUL CREATIVE AGENCY

THE BUSINESS GUIDE FOR GRAPHIC DESIGNERS, COPYWRITERS, FILMMAKERS, PHOTOGRAPHERS AND PROGRAMMERS

ANDY STROTE

CREATIVEAGENCYBOOK.COM

Dedicated to Marlene and Alex

CONTENTS

FOREWORD

Simon Burn, Co-founder, Fireworks Creative

I remember clearly when Andy and I founded Fireworks Creative. We had found a lovely space in Toronto's Fashion District. Andy's wife Marlene was an interior designer and she created a space full of bright, cheerful colors. It perfectly reflected the enthusiasm and positive energy for our new venture.

About one month in, having taken on our first employee, and having spent every day with Andy, I had made my first realization about him. He had a rather cool taste in shirts.

They were always something a little different from the norm; often edgy, creative, but always tasteful with noticeable attention to detail and of exceptional quality. It was clear he put a lot of thought into them, and always made an effort.

A year in, we had a few employees, and those sartorial traits carried through to the way he handled business, client projects, and people.

I've found many creative people tend to focus on themselves, and create things to impress their peers. This wasn't the case with Andy.

Every project we undertook, Andy would spend time to research and make sure he understood exactly what the purpose of the project was, or should be (often the client didn't know!), before we started coming up with solutions.

So many creative people have a predetermined idea of how a project should pan out, without putting much thought or effort into research or really understanding the project objectives.

They don't take the time to uncover how it fits in with the client's overall brand building and marketing objectives. Not Andy. I learnt a lot from working with him in this regard.

When our business grew, and new media choices came along, our agency quickly adapted to the changes.

Our positive attitude to embrace digital communications led us to become one of the first fully integrated media agencies in Canada. This was down to Andy's relentless pursuit of knowledge and a willingness to try new things.

As we took on more staff, we had HR issues to deal with. Again, Andy's willingness to listen, and problem-solving skills were very useful. He knew that people matter, and being kind and thoughtful towards others goes a long way.

Giving others the benefit of the doubt and showing empathy, putting in time to listen and guide; these traits are invaluable for building a multi-person business of any kind.

Over the years of working with Andy, I've learnt so much. When I read the first draft of this book, I got goose bumps. All that knowledge, wisdom and experience—crammed into these pages.

I can't think of another book or resource that will be as useful to help guide your journey through the creative world.

This book will help you build your career, deal with clients, and understand the business end of your creative agency. Even if you're a few years into your career, this is a must-read.

I can honestly say, I've learnt more from Andy than anyone else, and working with him has undoubtedly been a contributing factor in my own success.

Funnily enough though, I never developed a good sense for stylish shirts.

Simon Burn

Storyteller / Content Creator with a mouse and a camera

sdbcreative.com

Ben Hagon, Senior Designer, Context Creative

Andy and his business partner hired me as a senior designer in summer 2005. It was, and still is, the best job I ever had.

I had several offers at the time, but the choice was made easier when I had to drop by their office after work on a Friday. I found the team having cold beers and a whole bunch of laughs.

I had worked at two trendy Toronto design studios before, where awards, ego and reputation reigned. So to come to work at a modern communications agency, focused on client success and a progressive company culture, was to me, like a breath of fresh air.

That company ignited a spark in me. It showed me you could do good work and not be an asshole. It showed me the value of teamwork and collaboration. It showed me the value of being multi-disciplined.

And most importantly, it showed me what can happen when good people work hard at something.

I left the firm, due solely to a relocation. Andy and I kept in touch, and he offered much helpful advice as I started my own company.

I've carried many of the lessons learned into my own business, including a focus on client relationships, treating (and paying) people better than industry average, being multidisciplinary, and being an ethical and responsible company in both our words and actions.

I was thrilled to learn Andy was writing this book, and even more thrilled when he asked me to read the manuscript and write this foreword.

Contained within the book is more advice than can probably be absorbed, all learned and distilled over Andy's long career in creative communications.

It is a comprehensive guide to starting and running a creative agency. I truly wish I had a copy when I started mine.

Ben Hagon RGD

President and Creative Director

www.forgoodintent.com

PREFACE

I wrote this book in 2020/21 during the COVID-19 pandemic. Being an optimist, I assumed that one day soon the epidemic would be over. The world has faced plagues before, and eventually, they stop.

In this book, you'll find numerous mentions of meetings, networking, and other types of events where people gather. If you're reading this while the pandemic is still going on, you will have uncovered different ways to work with people at a distance, using more video conferencing, text, and email.

Just as I found it a good time for writing, I think it's also ideal for planning your next business move and the launch of your agency. Make use of these days. In the future, when your agency keeps you running hard, you'll look back and be thankful for the time you had to plan.

If you're reading this after the pandemic has passed, you may find yourself incorporating ways of working that became habits during the pandemic.

However, I would urge you to get as close and personal with your clients as you can. People work with people they know and trust, and that's all based on tight relationships.

Note that my recommendations are from my experience in business and are not intended to be professional advice. Always consult with a lawyer, accountant, or any other professional for your specific needs.

IS THIS BOOK FOR YOU?

"The average introduction to almost any book is somewhat of a bore"

— Boris Karloff

This book is for people who want to start their own agency to provide content and creative services to marketing and advertising clients.

That includes graphic designers, copywriters, filmmakers, photographers, photo editors, film editors, animators, illustrators, interface designers, and front-end programmers.

In this book, I will help you build a solid business foundation for your company.

I'll teach you about running your business so that you can focus your creativity on what you really love doing, whether that's writing, designing, filmmaking, programming—whatever area of creative services you're pursuing. You might be 14, 24, 34, or 54— your age doesn't matter.

You may be studying design in school with little or no practical business experience. Perhaps you didn't go to college or university for this. Maybe you've been an amateur photographer since you were 14, and now you want to make it your business.

You may be working in another field and creating content as a side hustle to get yourself into the business. Some of you may be employed by a design or advertising firm and are thinking of going out on your own.

Perhaps you're an independent freelancer wondering whether it's time to grow your business. Perhaps you've already taken the leap and started a bigger agency.

Wherever you are in life, this book will give you practical advice to run your creative agency efficiently and profitably.

Some chapters of the book may not apply to you. In that case, just skip them. You can cherry-pick which chapters to read or read them in any order you like.

What This Book *Won't* Do for You

This book will *not* teach you graphic design, copywriting, photography, filmmaking, programming, or other creative skills. I'm assuming that you are either learning your craft or are already able to deliver your services at a professional level.

What this book *will* do is guide you on the business side so that running your agency doesn't overwhelm your creativity. Many creative agencies struggle or fail, not because their creative output wasn't good enough, but because their owners didn't know how to operate a business.

As a business owner, you have to excel at both your craft and business operations. It may not come naturally to you, but you can learn. I did it, and so can you.

. . .

My Background

I have been a copywriter, creative director, and owner of three creative agencies in Toronto.

I've worked as an employee for six different ad agencies, large and small.

For many years after that, I was a solopreneur in my first agency, Red Line Design. I worked from home, providing freelance copywriting services.

That business was so successful I knew I needed more resources, so I started Fireworks Creative, my first fully integrated creative agency. I found a compatible business partner, and in five years, we grew Fireworks Creative from the two of us to 30 people. We worked for some of Canada's most prominent corporate and government clients.

Soon we were on the radar of two large companies interested in buying our firm.

We were pursued by Havas, a global advertising network (they flew us to New York for a meeting—how exciting!) and also Cognicase, a multinational IT company based in Montreal. We chose to sell to Cognicase for $3 million.

Six months later, I was asked to leave (very typical for those kinds of deals), and after a summer of thinking about next steps, I started Context Creative with one partner and one employee.

We grew that company to 28 people. After 15 years, it was time for a change, and I sold my shares to my partners. Context Creative still operates successfully today.

I've created communications in all media, including web, social media, email, video, TV, radio, print, and billboards. I've created content with designers, art directors, photographers, filmmakers, animators, illustrators, programmers, and many other creative service providers.

I've hired people, fired people, and had to let good people go during a business downturn.

Through all of this, I've learned the nitty-gritty of running a business. That includes finding the best clients and the most practical ways to work with staff and partners. Some of this I learned the easy way, and some the painful way.

When you start your agency, you'll undoubtedly run into a few bumps in the road. But it will be a much smoother ride if you follow the advice in this book.

1

STARTING YOUR OWN CREATIVE AGENCY

"The secret to getting ahead is getting started."

— Mark Twain

Starting a Business: It's the Best of Times, It's the Worst of Times

Today is both the best and worst time to get into the creative agency business. Technology and our general understanding of work have changed in many ways over the last few years.

Some of these changes provide opportunities we didn't have before, while others make it more challenging to start a business.

Here's why it's the best:

- The Internet: We take it for granted, but just think about it. This is your vehicle for communications and collaboration, your file sharing and storage depot, your portfolio, your entertainment, and finally, where most of your work will be experienced.

- Mobility and connectivity: You can work from a coffee shop anywhere in the world.
- You can work with people located anywhere. You're able to take advantage of time zones—you can have people around the world working for you while you're sleeping. That's huge!
- Today, big clients accept working with smaller companies. You don't have to be a conglomerate. They'll hire you for your talent. It wasn't always that way.
- Powerful equipment is dirt cheap. You can make a film on your phone, edit it on your laptop, and get it in front of a global audience free of charge. Incredible!
- The world is undergoing massive changes. Change creates opportunities. If you can ride the wave, there's never been a better time.

Here's why it's the worst:

- The Internet: Now your competition is global. There are content creators living in countries that you can't find on a map. They're competing to design logos for $10, where you might typically charge $5,000.
- At the top end of the business, multinational consulting companies are getting into the creative agency business. They're trying to cream off the best most profitable clients.
- Thousands of creative individuals, just like you, are thinking of doing exactly what you're doing.
- Free or cheap stock photography and video clips are everywhere, and soon AI will be writing social media and websites.
- The world is undergoing massive changes. Change

creates confusion and turmoil, and you can easily get swept away.

So, take your pick. Is it the best or worst time?

Actually, it's not a choice. It's all true.

Why Do You Want Your Own Company?

Before we look at your motives for starting your own company, let's first see whether I can discourage you from starting one altogether.

Consider the following:

- Statistics show that about 20 percent of small businesses fail in their first year.
- About 50 percent fail within five years. People lose a lot of money; many declare bankruptcy. It's not pretty.
- Running a company means you're responsible for all kinds of administrative tasks, managing employees, and doing 101 things you don't like and are probably not naturally good at either.
- Most aspects of your business will take you away from what you like to do, whether that's writing, designing, photographing, or programming.
- All the money worries of the company are now your worries. How well do you sleep?
- You have to get comfortable presenting your work in front of a boardroom full of clients. Your company's success may depend on it. Can you do that? Or do you freeze with stage fright? Regardless, you have no choice.
- If you're good at your craft, you might make more money being an employee without the headaches of running a company. Why not just do that?

Okay, if you're not totally discouraged, let me guess why you might want to run your own show:

- You are or want to be an entrepreneur, and you think you have a better idea for an agency.
- You've already been working on your own, and you're so busy that you need more people to take care of clients. So, you're thinking of forming a bigger company. (That's my story.)
- You're currently an employee, you've watched how agencies do business, and you think that now it's time for your own.
- You think you can make much more money if it's your company.
- You started with content creation as a side hustle. It's growing like crazy, and you're convinced that now is the time to make it a real company.
- You've developed a massive personal following on social media, and you think you could do that for corporate clients too.
- You've been working as a team with another freelancer, and she suggested you go into business together.
- And many other reasons I haven't considered.

Before You Start, Ask Yourself This One Question

The question is simple. Here it is: for you, is starting your own company a HELL YEAH, or a NO?[1]

Do you have an absolute burning desire to do this? Have you been thinking about it, planning, reading, talking to friends and family about it? If you're not 110 percent obsessed with it, maybe it's not a HELL YEAH. In that case, it's a NO. There's no in-between.

Don't start a company if it's something you're kinda, sorta, maybe considering. It's far easier to be an employee without all of the worries of running a business. You'll have more fun, more flexibility, and sleep better most nights.

But if it's a HELL YEAH! then let's get going...

Your Current Situation and Your Options

Take a few moments to consider where you are in life, where you want to go in the content creation business, and what you could do right now to get there faster. Let's look at a few possible situations:

- You're in high school and think you want to work in the content creation field. Could you get a summer or part-time job in the industry? Do you know anyone who would let you be a helper, doing odd jobs? Are you working on your own projects? Now is an excellent time to create your first portfolio.
- You're in college studying in a relevant field. You have many options: do your own projects, create a product or service you can sell, get a part-time/summer job in the industry, take a business course in summer school, or concentrate on building a network through social media.
- You finished college with a degree in a relevant creative services field. Ideally, you've landed an internship or a job in the industry. If not, work on networking through social media. Get some freelance clients, and when you're ready, start your own company.
- You've started working at a company in a relevant field. Do

great work, exceed your boss's expectations, keep your eyes and ears open and learn the business. Get some freelance clients. Think about how you'd like your career to evolve.

- You're working, but not in a creative services field, and want to make a switch. Start a content creation business as a side hustle. Your goal is to grow it into a full-time agency.
- You've started your company. Keep focused on getting the right clients, being profitable, setting goals, and meeting them.

Start Building a Professional Online Profile Now

Even if you're still a student, or you're thinking of starting a company in a few years, now is the time to begin building your professional online profile. Keep it separate from your personal one. Your personal accounts may be on Instagram or TikTok. Make your professional profile on LinkedIn.

As soon as you start working in any capacity, whether you're looking for an internship or pitching freelance clients, your LinkedIn profile can act as your résumé and portfolio.

It may seem a bit old school and boring, but it's where business lives today. Take the time to learn all of LinkedIn's capabilities and use them.

Make LinkedIn your showcase. Remember, you can post updates, including graphics and videos that are visible to all of your connections and anyone who looks for you. You can participate in discussions and ask questions. You can network with people in companies where you're looking for an introduction.

In the past, it was often tough to get through to decision-makers. LinkedIn makes it much easier. As a bonus, LinkedIn performs very well in search engines. Search anyone's name, and their LinkedIn profile will usually be near the top.

Chapter Takeaways

- If you want to start your creative agency, be sure that you're fully committed. It's not a casual decision.
- Whatever your current status, try to get as close to the business as you can. Read blogs and newsletters, subscribe to podcasts, monitor and participate in social media.
- Start building your online profile on LinkedIn and creating a network. This takes time, so start now.

---

1. Buy and read *Hell Yeah or No: What's Worth Doing* by Derek Sivers (New York: Hit Media, 2020). It's a short but inspiring book.

2

TAKING ADVANTAGE OF SCHOOL

"No thief, however skillful, can rob one of knowledge, and that is why knowledge is the best and safest treasure to acquire."

— L. Frank Baum

Going to School for This? Make the Most of It

Whether you're going to a college or university right after high school, or you're doing this later in life, take advantage of being in full-time learning mode. You may never have this opportunity again. This is the time to work your butt off, live on coffee and adrenaline, and start producing a great portfolio.

It's also a time to begin figuring out what you want to do within your line of work. You don't have to make any firm decisions, and you can always change directions later, but you might already get a feel for what appeals to you.

For example, if you're studying photography, you'll want to learn everything about the craft and try different areas. But maybe you already know that your biggest interest is fashion photography, or automotive, or portraits. If you're lucky, you'll get to experiment with everything while you're in school.

A word of caution: if you're just slouching through school, barely getting a passing grade, not sure whether you want to be there, may I suggest that either you reconsider what you're doing with your life or quit school and start your career without the benefit of the education.

Remember, once you're out of school, you'll be up against the best new graduates from around the world. The competition will be tough, so make sure you're ready for it.

Be Your Teachers' Pet

Your teachers are there to help you develop your skills in your area of study, to challenge you, guide you, and answer your questions.

But there's another job your teachers can do for you that is equally important, and it comes toward the end of your last school year.

Your teachers can have a tremendous impact on the start of your career by introducing you to industry insiders, recommending you, and getting you a paid internship at a top company.

I cannot overemphasize how important this is. In your final year of school, your focus should be to create a spectacular portfolio of work so that your teachers can help you land a high-level intern placement. Make sure you're on their radar. Ask for feedback on your portfolio, and get information on the various placements that may be available.

This is no time to be the quiet, mousy kid. Get in there and get some attention.

Put Your Teachers' Connections to Work for You

Maybe you haven't given much thought to your teachers' backgrounds. Most teachers have worked in the business and have maintained contacts there. They've established first-name relationships with company owners, creative directors, and others who might hire their students.

If you've ever had guest lecturers come into your classrooms to speak to you, they likely got there because your teachers knew them.

Many teachers also keep in touch with the industry at design conferences, awards shows, and other events. Your job is to make sure that your teachers work for you when it comes time to intern.

Starting at the Top Is Much, Much Easier

Getting the right internship can be such a head start for your career. If you get into a top company, you'll be with the best people in the industry, collaborating with smart, experienced clients.

You'll be pushed to produce your strongest work. You might put in insane hours, but you'll be completely absorbed in your assignments. In no time, you'll have a professional portfolio that will take you to even greater heights.

What's the alternative? You'll get an internship at some "creative factory," where they crank out junk mail that goes right into everyone's recycling bin. It's the same grind every week. You'll wonder why you wanted to be in this business.

But as discouraging as that might sound from the creative side, you can still turn it into a valuable experience. You can observe how the owners run their business, manage each project, and handle clients.

Some of those creative factories have the best systems in place for turning out work efficiently—pay attention!

Even if you're not learning much on the creative side, make the most of it and learn something about running the business.

How Creative Agencies See Interns

Toward the end of every school year, agencies and corporate communications departments get bombarded by emails, texts, social media contacts, and unsolicited portfolios from interns looking for a placement.

Generally, a smaller company can only handle one intern at a time. Larger ones might take on a few more.

As an intern, you have to understand that while you're doing either paid or unpaid work for the company, you're also costing the company. It takes time to show you how things are done and get you to produce something that can be presented to a client. That's time the company has to invest in you.

In business, time is money. And just when you've got the hang of it, the internship is over, and their investment in you disappears.

Realistically, many companies take on interns to do their part and give back to the industry. It's generally a myth that interns are cheap labor. For the company, taking on an intern is often a small step away from charity. So, when interns come knocking, the response frequently is, "No, sorry, we're not taking interns this year."

But the teacher's call can break through all of that. Here's how it goes:

Teacher: "Hi, Bob. Were you planning to take on any interns this season?"

Creative Director Bob: "Oh, I don't know, not sure yet..."

Teacher: "Listen, I've got this kid here, who is so good, I think you should see her. Her portfolio looks like someone who's been in the business for years. The work is clean, and she's a good thinker. Can you make time to see her? She'd be a good fit for you guys."

Creative Director Bob: "Yeah, okay. How about next Tuesday? What's her name?"

You want to be that "kid." Your teacher has to know who you are, and your work has to be top-notch. No teacher will put their credibility on the line for a mediocre student. Then you have to show up and ace the interview.

While some internships happen mid-term, the critical ones occur toward the end of your schooling. This is your chance to get an internship that turns into a full-time job.

In my agencies we hired many, but not all, of our interns to stay on full time.

Should You Take an Unpaid Internship?

The easy answer is no; you should not take on an unpaid position. It's unethical and exploitive. The graphic designers' associations in North America have come out strongly against it. So, just say no. That's the industry position.

Is there any possible reason to say yes? Yes, there is. If you don't need the money, if you genuinely believe you can talk your way into a paying job there, if you know someone there who will help you either move up at the company or move out into a paying position, you might consider it.

Just keep in mind that this is not normal, and in the end, you may feel exploited. While I don't recommend taking an unpaid internship, it's a personal decision.

An Internship on the Client Side? Could Be a Great Idea!

Many corporations have significant internal communications departments. This is especially true of larger traditional companies such as banks, insurance, telecommunications, accounting, professional consulting firms, etc.

These companies usually also work with one or more outside agencies, design firms, and photographers. The work tends to get divided up—some is handled internally, other work goes out to their suppliers.

Exactly how it's divided varies by company, but the internal department typically takes care of social media, website updates, newsletters, everyday PowerPoint presentations, and other graphic requirements.

Depending on what you're looking for, this can be a valuable internship. Here's what you'll learn there:

- Organization: These companies will have systems and bureaucracy set up for everything. Not that you'll necessarily want to emulate it, but when you start your own company, you'll know a systematic way of working.
- Depending on how the company operates, you may have an opportunity to interact with both internal clients and outside agencies, and other suppliers. You'll see different sides of the business that you wouldn't otherwise see.
- You may also learn that many big corporations operate in a more nine-to-five mentality. If you ever want to work on your own or as a supplier, you're best to forget that. You'll be working longer hours if you're working outside

of these companies. But, while you're there, you might find time to start up your side hustle freelance business.

Try to Turn Your Internship into a Full-Time Job

Ideally, you want to get an internship at a company where you'd like to work full time. In other words, at the end of your internship period, you want them to hire you. As an intern, your goal is to be such a superstar that they want to keep you around and start paying you a good salary. Why?

First, it's so much easier. You've just spent weeks, maybe months learning about how this company works and the types of jobs they do. Your internship will go by fast, and it would be ideal if you could put that experience to work and carry on at the same company.

Second, imagine you've done an eight-week internship. You're just getting to know everyone, you feel like you've joined the industry, and already it's over, and you're out again.

Now you have to start on the job hunt, having had a little internship experience but no real employee experience. While it would be ideal to stay on, realistically, the company may not need more full-time staff.

In that case, you want to make sure you get a warm letter of recommendation from the creative director that you can show at interviews.

Ideally, the creative director will also agree to act as a reference for you. That means you can put their name and contact information on your résumé and be confident that if someone contacts them, they'll say nice things about you.

Also, ask them whether they can recommend anyone for you to call. Contacting companies will be so much easier when you can say that "Creative Director Bob" suggested I call you. That's very important when you start. Many creative directors know each other, so a personal reference carries some weight.

Getting an Internship in a "Glamor Business"

For many people in the creative fields, their ideal internship would be in fashion, travel, feature films, television, or food. And while there are often internships available, in many cases, the more glamorous the business, the less they pay, if they pay at all.

Why? Two reasons: first, so many people want to get in, they have their choice, and that often means an offer of an unpaid internship. They know that someone will take it. So, it can be very exploitive.

Second, aside from all the perceived glamor, many of these businesses operate on incredibly tight budgets. There just isn't that much money in them—certainly not to pay good salaries to interns.

Some of these companies are known for offering unpaid internships that turn into low-paying jobs for the alleged "high profile, fun, and glamor." Meanwhile, you'd have to work a second job to buy groceries.

People are doing very well financially in all of those businesses. But they're generally owners, partners, and executives, not the lower rungs of the creative services area. So, if those are the businesses you're interested in, go in with your eyes open.

Thinking of Starting Your Own Creative Agency Right Out of School, or With No School at All?

Let's assume you decide to skip the internship or getting a job working for someone else. What if you want to start your agency right out of school? Or what if you didn't go to school for this at all but have been a creator for many years and now want to make it your living?

You've likely heard stories about other young entrepreneurs who turned their talent into a career at a very young age. They didn't work for someone else; they took the express elevator right to the top of the industry—from child genius to superstar.

Maybe they were making videos on YouTube for a few years, and then they made a few commercials for small businesses owned by friends. One job led to another, and today they're making a good living working for major advertisers.

You might have heard the story about the guy who talked his way into a big ad agency as a copywriter at age 17, and by 23, was the creative director for the whole agency. Yes, it does happen, but not often. It's like winning the lottery.

If you think you're cut out for that route, read the sections of the book on how to run your business so you don't get bogged down by the admin side of work.

For most creators, I recommend getting real-world experience working in someone else's company before going out on your own. It's so much easier to learn from others, and it can help you avoid making every possible mistake along the way.

Also, the company will likely have much more impressive clients than you'll get when you're starting on your own. That means your portfolio will be filled with recognizable names and likely more significant projects than you would otherwise have.

The Biggest Challenges Starting Your Business When You're Young

You're going to face many challenges when you start your business, but you can overcome them. The first challenge will simply be your age. You'll have to compensate for that.

You could be working with clients in their forties, fifties, and sixties, and you'll find yourself in the position of making recommendations to them. As you sit there thinking, "Hey, this guy is older than my parents," the client guy is thinking, "This kid is younger than my kids. Why should I be listening to him?"

It's not only the age difference but also the accompanying difference in experience and practice. Unless you're there just to take orders from the client and execute them, you're coming up with ideas that you're going to have to sell.

Chances are, the client has far more experience than you do. He's done something like this for 20 years. You're in your first year of business.

It gets especially tricky when the client asks for something that you don't think is a good idea. In fact, it's precisely the opposite of how you wanted to handle it.

This is where your maturity, diplomatic skills, and negotiating skills come in. How do you deal with that?

Spoiler: you do it both ways. You agree to do it their way, but also negotiate to be able to show your version. You will pledge to put in equal amounts of effort to make both concepts work, and you will be happy when they choose either version.

During all of this, you'll have to be very confident in what you propose, how you manage your work, how you present it, and how you take in feedback.

Your presentation skills and your ability to convince a client, while respecting and integrating their feedback, will be critical. You have to ask yourself whether you can handle this. There will be pressure, and you'll be worried about whether you can live up to the client's expectations.

The Best Opening When You're Young: The Latest Trend

If you're young and lucky, you are going into the marketplace riding the latest, greatest trend where no one has much experience. It's the one time when everyone will listen to young people because:

1. Young people are always the first to know about the latest cool stuff.
2. Older people have no choice because they don't know anything about it.

When the web became commercialized, it was hobbyist coders who built the first big websites. I worked with an 18-year-old guy who didn't go to university because he was in such demand as a coder and figured university would be a waste of time. (He was right. Today, he runs a very successful company.)

When Facebook started accepting ads... When Pinterest became known as a way of driving traffic... When Shopify became famous... When TikTok came along... These were all opportunities for young people to lead, mainly because no one else had any experience.

So, look around. What's a new and exciting trend or technology you can learn, excel at, promote, and sell? Who would be the target audience, and how will you reach them?

Every new technology or platform has early adopters who break ground, bringing the corporate world along. It can be a very profitable way to enter the market.

Chapter Takeaways

- If you're going to school, make the most of it. Get close to your teachers and get their help to land the best internship possible.
- If you get an internship, try to get hired at the end of it. It will make things so much easier.
- If you're not going to school, consider becoming an expert in the latest, greatest trend. It's the one time that everyone will listen to a young person's advice because you know something they don't.

3

AMATEUR CREATOR VS. PROFESSIONAL

"A professional is a man who can do his job when he doesn't feel like it; an amateur is one who can't when he does feel like it. "

— James Agate

Working for Yourself vs. Working for Clients—There are Important Differences

If you're not doing paying work for clients, you're an amateur. Before you get offended by the negative implication, let's look at the definition of "amateur." An amateur is someone who engages in a pursuit, study, science, or sport as a pastime rather than as a profession.

So, it doesn't necessarily mean that you're not good at what you're doing. It only means you haven't turned pro.

How does that translate in the world of content creation? Let's look at videos. You might see a video on YouTube with production values as good as any corporate commercial, but someone created it for their own pleasure and their followers.

No one paid them to do it other than maybe YouTube if the channel is monetized with enough followers.

This is an important fact to understand—in many cases, the difference between amateur and professional is not the quality of the product. The video could meet the highest standards, but it's still amateur. It was created for the love of filmmaking.

So, if it's not the quality of the creative, what are the differences between amateur and professional? There are a few points to consider:

1. The first big difference is that amateurs are creating for themselves. As an amateur, you're self-directed. If you're making a video, no one tells you what to do, and you're not working to someone else's requirements.
2. You're choosing the subject matter and how to shoot and edit it. You can decide whether or not you want to create a storyboard for yourself before you shoot.
3. You're in charge of the sound and music choices. You can make whatever changes you like to suit your vision—no one else will ever know.
4. You can take as long as you want. The schedule is up to you.
5. You're not creating for a specific result, such as driving more product sales or pushing traffic to a particular website. Your goal in making a video to play on YouTube is to get better at your craft and attract views, likes, comments, and more followers.

Perhaps, if you get enough traffic, you'll get the attention of sponsors who will pay you.

If you're outstanding and work very hard at it, you could get enough viewers so that your combined income from YouTube and sponsors is enough to make a living. That becomes your job

—keep making videos to attract eyeballs to keep the numbers up.

I know many filmmakers who are trying to do precisely that. They are working on getting hundreds of thousands or millions of followers, which is enough to earn a living.

Most of them don't have any ambition to work for clients who dictate what they do; they are happy making their videos and trying to get paid for it.

But, of course, that only works for a tiny percentage of YouTube filmmakers. The vast majority are not making a living at it. They are happy to keep filmmaking as a hobby and lucky if they're getting a little bit from YouTube and the occasional sponsor.

I know other filmmakers are trying to use YouTube as a stepping stone to becoming a professional director, making commercials for paying clients.

What Does It Mean to Be a Professional?

As a professional, you're working to someone else's specifications, timelines, and budgets.

Imagine you're a filmmaker, and you've been introduced to the owner of a local pizzeria who would like a short, exciting video to run on Facebook. You figure you can handle this on your own, or perhaps get a friend to help you.

Once you understand what the client is looking for, you'll have to give them an estimate and a timeline for the work. Or they may tell you how much budget they have for this production.

Let's assume you agree on the fee, and they sign off. Then, you'll meet with them to review what they have in mind for the spot.

You may learn that they have some shots that they consider critical, like a hot pizza coming out of their new Italian oven and the sign on the window. While you're there, you'll roughly block out the shots you're going to need.

You will create a script and storyboard for the client to sign off on, as well as a schedule that will keep you on track. The script includes a bit of voice-over with music and sound effects, so you don't have to worry about any on-camera talent or recording live audio.

Since you're shooting this in their shop, you'll have to schedule the shoot after they close, so you'll be starting at two in the morning.

The client will be there while you're shooting and may have some suggestions as you work. You'll need to either accommodate them or diplomatically convince the client that what you're doing is best for the spot.

Let's say everything goes well. You get all the footage you need, and the client seems happy as you wrap up just before noon. Now you'll get a friend who is a proven voice talent to record your announcer audio for you. Then, you'll spend a few hours choosing the perfect music and sound effects. Finally, you'll take two days to edit it, remembering to put in the required graphics.

At last, you're ready to show the client your first cut. If you're lucky, they'll love every second of it. On the other hand, there may be one or two things they'd like you to change. Fortunately, the changes are easy and don't require any additional shooting.

With that, you put the final touches on the video and send the file to the client. The client texts you to say he's thrilled! Thank you very much! With a smile on your face, you write up an invoice and send it along.

Let's stop for a minute to review your hours. You had the initial meeting with the client, followed by another one to present the storyboard.

Then you spent the night shooting. You spent two days on music, sound effects, and editing. A few revisions took a couple of hours. You should give your friend something for his work on the voice recording.

Roughly, you spent the better part of a week on this project, with your time on the job plus a bit of running around. How much do you charge?

Let's run through some imaginary numbers. Imagine you charged $1,500 for this week. If you're able to get two jobs like this every month, which isn't easy to do, that's about $36,000 a year. How does that feel?

Okay, let's imagine you could charge twice as much—$3,000 for a one-week job. Again, assuming you could get two a month, that's $72,000 a year. That's better, right? But will you be able to find enough projects that will pay you an average of $3,000 for a week of your time and talent?

It's worthwhile to run these numbers through your head. Think of a day rate or a week rate. How much do you want for a day or week of your time? How hard will you have to work to make a living that makes you happy? Where will you find the clients that will keep you consistently busy?

One last point: realistically, if you do get this busy—an average of one job every two weeks—you may need the help of an assistant, perhaps part-time or as needed. That means that whatever you're billing, some of that will have to go to the assistant.

You could take the pressure off earning a full-time living from this and consider it a side hustle. Even so, how much would you charge to feel that you've been fairly compensated?

I don't have any stock answers to these questions. You need to answer them for yourself if you're thinking of doing projects like this, either full-time or as a side hustle.

Take time to consider the kinds of projects you see yourself doing, how much effort would be required, and what you'd want to charge. Although I used the making of a commercial as an example, the same applies to writers, designers, photographers, and programmers.

By the way, I'm not recommending you do what I just described. As you'll see, I think you'd be far better off following a different path. I used this example only because I see so many creators going in this direction. It's a hard way to make a living. I'll show you much better ways.

A Professional Director Working for Large Clients

I know some filmmakers see themselves shooting big-budget commercials for cars, travel, and national brands. From there, the next logical level would be directing films.

Perhaps the best-known example of this is Ridley Scott, who successfully transitioned from directing commercials to making feature films like *Alien*, *Gladiator*, and *Thelma & Louise*.

Working at that level is an entirely different story than doing a spot for the local pizzeria or coffee shop. You'll only get there as a director with a great reel of commercials, shot over many years.

You're now competing on a global scale. For the biggest commercials, it's not unusual for directors to work anywhere in the world.

At this level, you are working with a production company hired by the advertising agency that does the work for the client.

In other words, when it comes down to the job, you're working with the production company crew for your immediate client, which is the agency. It's the agency that created the script and is working with you to deliver the spot to the end client.

In all likelihood, the agency will give you a briefing that includes a storyboard and script that the client has approved. They may have precedents of previous commercials for a shooting and editing style. They want a new commercial, but it may have to fit within an existing campaign look.

On the business side, you'll have to provide the production company with a detailed estimate for your services. You may be bidding on the job against other directors.

So, even though you may have attended one or more briefing meetings and spent many hours coming up with the estimate, the project isn't necessarily yours.

But let's say you win the job. You review the storyboard, and you have some ideas that you think would improve it. Working with the production company and the agency, you'll have a chance to present your ideas.

For elements such as music and sound design, the agency will likely have picked another production company they want to use so that you would be working with them. You'll have meetings with them to ensure that everything lines up.

You may or may not have your choice of editors—that depends on the arrangement with the production company. Once you're finished shooting, after the footage has been reviewed, you may not see the commercial until it's finished.

I've worked on commercials where the director was off to the next job once the shoot was over. The production company finished it and showed him the first cut. He could add input, but his job was done.

Working Arrangements for Freelance Directors, Programmers, Designers, and Writers

The way individual creators work for clients varies, generally depending on the type and size of the client. For small businesses, most creators will work directly with the clients.

Whether you're directing commercials, producing or managing social media, programming, designing, or writing, you're likely meeting with the end client, possibly the business owner.

Even at this level, which tends to be less formal, you should follow standard operating procedures. Read the sections on creating detailed estimates, invoices, and terms of payment.

You don't need to go overboard on paperwork, but you want enough to make sure you're covered, get the job done smoothly, and get paid.

Once you move up to larger clients, the working arrangements often change. That's because these clients have in-house marketing departments that tend to have relationships with ad agencies, PR companies, and design studios, in addition to individual freelancers.

Here's one way of looking at it: the bigger the project, where more people are needed to complete it, the more likely an agency or studio does it.

So, if you're working on your own and want to have these types of clients and projects, you may have to get hired by the agency, perhaps freelance or on contract. That's particularly true for directors and programmers.

However, you may still be able to work directly with the client on projects that one person can easily handle, such as writing. When I was working solo freelance, I did a lot of writing for big compa-

nies with in-house marketing departments. It was these departments that hired me.

In-house marketing departments like to have several suppliers on
hand so they can pick and choose and control the projects themselves. They work with graphic designers in a similar fashion.

But, for the largest projects, they would look to their ad agency or
studios. For example, they wouldn't give a significant website
design and programming to an individual programmer. They
would see it as too risky and feel more reassured going to a larger
company.

The same would apply to a commercial—they would likely go to
a bigger company for the various types of expertise required for
the job.

As an independent freelancer, you need to know that you're likely
wasting your time trying to work directly with big clients on
significant projects that require larger teams.

You either won't get the projects at all, or the client may pair you
up with their ad agency, design studio, or production company.
However, you may still get smaller projects, and a steady stream
of those projects is plenty to keep you busy.

Chapter Takeaways

- There's a big difference between doing your own projects
  and working at a professional level. As a professional, it's
  your clients who call the shots.
- If you plan to start with small clients, think about who
  you want to work with, how you'll attract them, and how
  much you can charge.
- It's essential to understand who you're working for. As

you move up to more significant projects, you may not be working for the actual client. Your client may be an ad agency, design studio, or production company.

4

GETTING A JOB—YOU'RE IN THE BUSINESS

"That's when I first learned that it wasn't enough to just do your job, you had to have an interest in it, even a passion for it."

— Charles Bukowski

How to Rock Your First Job

You've made it past the internship and landed a job. Congratulations, you're in the business! If you're fortunate, you're at a top firm working shoulder-to-shoulder with the best. If not, don't give up. There is still a lot for you to learn, not only about your actual craft but about how a business runs.

Wherever you are, for the first year, your head will likely be spinning. It is so different from school, and you'll find yourself in many new situations. That's okay. Everyone knows you're new and still learning. Don't be afraid to ask for help from more senior members of the team.

For your business development, this is the time to get real-world experience and observe how the company works. You'll most likely be in an open studio environment, which gives you the chance to overhear a lot of what's going on.

Think of your job as your next-level teacher, where they're paying you while you're learning—take advantage of it.

Be a Sponge—Absorb Everything

In addition to learning and improving your craft, you need to take this opportunity to learn the business side of things. Here are a few things to pay attention to:

- Watch for and listen to how the business operates. How do they open up a new project? Do they use software to track jobs and hours? Which software?
- Have a look at how they estimate projects. Study an estimate. How do they describe what they propose to deliver to the client?
- Observe how they manage projects through the different phases. Watch how they get from client briefing to studio briefing, concept development, internal presentation, client presentation, client feedback, changes/alterations, final client approval, creating the final files, and potentially working with other suppliers to deliver the completed job.
- Pay attention to how they work with outside partners and suppliers. Depending on the type of work, this could be anyone from programming specialists, recording studios, photographers, or video production houses.
- Ideally, they will have processes, aka Standard Operating Procedures, for how they run their business. That's what you'll want for your company, a consistent way of doing things.
- Or you may be on the other side of the equation, as a member of the video crew and learning how to work as a

supplier to ad agencies or direct clients. Wherever you fit into this picture, pay attention to everything happening around you. If possible, get yourself invited to meetings to observe the interactions.

Being able to work smoothly with collaborators and clients is critical. When you start your own business, you'll have to know how to ensure that you deliver solid projects as a team.

In this business, you're only as good as your last project, and a client is free to find other suppliers at any time. Every job is important, and every detail matters.

A Good Project Manager Will Keep You Sane

Most companies have someone to see jobs through. They could be called project managers, account managers, operations managers, or administrative assistants.

They initiate projects, help the creative people prioritize their workloads, and make sure everyone meets deadlines. They also ensure that the creative director vets everything well ahead of client presentation time.

Along the way, the project manager tracks all related costs so that the job gets billed accurately. Once it's over, they check to see that any relevant files are correctly archived.

You may be surprised how often you go back to archived files to reuse something in a new project. Learn how to archive files properly.

You can learn a lot from project managers. They are the ones taking care of the business side of the company. They are the glue holding everything together.

When you have your own company and grow beyond two or three people, your project managers will be critical to your success.

Also, pay attention to how the studio handles the creative part of the job. In some studios, they assign a project to one person or team. In other studios, they have internal competitions, giving the same project to several people and then sorting out the best ideas to present to the client.

Watch for the creative director's involvement. Some are very hands-on, while others mostly supervise. One day, when you're running your own business, you'll be in charge of creative. Think about how you see yourself working in that role.

No matter how the creative teams work, it will likely be the project manager who reminds everyone about deadlines and reviews the deliverables to make sure nothing has been missed. So, talk to your project managers and learn as you go.

Always Do More Than What Your Boss Asks For

This is the time to show initiative and work hard. Let's say you're a graphic designer in a creative agency, and you've been assigned to redesign an existing website.

For your briefing, you've received all the information you need. Based on that, they've asked you to come up with three rough design concepts for an internal presentation in a few days.

Perhaps another designer has been given the same assignment so that during the internal review, there will be at least six designs to consider. The agency has promised to show three options to the client, so these six ideas will be revised and whittled down to three final concepts.

Your first job here is to do precisely what was asked of you. But realize that coming up with the three ideas is the minimum expectation. If you want to shine, you need to deliver more.

Aside from your three concepts, do you have additional ideas? What about variations of details such as colors, typography, illustration, or photo styles? How about options for navigation and menu behavior? Did you do screen grabs of other websites to find ideas that might be suitable for this project?

Whatever the assignment, whatever your role in the project, don't forget that what they've asked you to do is just enough for you to keep your job. It is the very least that's expected.

To stand out from the crowd, you have to over-deliver. Aside from making sure you get noticed, it's simply a good exercise. You're a creative person, aren't you? This is the time to show what you're capable of and stretch your creative muscles.

Of all the designers who worked in our agencies over the years, I can remember the ones who rose above the basic demands and always came with additional ideas for consideration. Your boss will remember too.

It's Showtime—Your First Presentation to a Client

When you're a junior in the firm, you may not be invited to client presentations or meetings for quite a while. But at some point, you'll be asked into one of these meetings, perhaps just to observe.

And then will come a day when the creative director says, "Do you want to present your concepts?"

I can tell you, the first few times you have to get up in a boardroom to take clients through your work is nerve-wracking. You might get stage fright. You might start to ramble and lose your train of thought. You'll need a glass of water.

If you're smart, you will have rehearsed this so that you'll know what you're going to say and what will be left for others to say. On the other hand, some people are natural presenters.

If you have any similar experience, for example, doing stand-up comedy, playing in a band, or acting in theatre, this may come easier for you. But for most people, it takes practice to get comfortable standing at the front of a boardroom with all eyes on you.

Being able to present creative work convincingly is a critical skill to learn. You may even want to take some coaching in this area.

In most major cities there are many independent presentation coaches, sometimes called speaker's coaches. You'll also find well-known companies such as Toastmasters and the Dale Carnegie organization, where you can learn to polish your presentations.

Once you've started your own company, you'll be the senior person and will be doing a lot of presenting. Get good at it.

Moving to Your Second Job

Assuming you like your first job and it's going well, you should start thinking about moving to your next job sometime after two years.

However, if you've made a colossal mistake taking that first job and know that this is just not for you, start looking sooner. Not every company is right for every person, and vice versa.

Why should you think about moving on after two years if everything is going well? Here's why:

1. After two years, you should have worked on a variety of projects that the company usually produces. By that time, you get it. Unless they frequently bring in new clients, you will have seen the range of work available there.

2. You will have learned how this company operates, whether you agree with all of it or not.

3. You will have made new friends and acquaintances. Keep these people close to you. Add them to your LinkedIn network. They don't have to become your best friends; they can be your "business friends."

4. When you move on, you may find that the next company operates entirely differently. It's helpful for you to see other ways of doing business.

5. But here's the key reason for moving—you'll make more money. Staying at the same company, you'll likely get an annual review and an incremental raise in pay. The only way to make a significant salary jump is to go somewhere else and ask for more. If your work justifies it, they'll pay.

6. Of course, you want to make sure you have a firm contract in writing with the new company before giving notice. Generally, the minimum is two weeks' notice, but they may ask you to stay longer. But also be prepared for them to ask you to leave immediately. It could happen. You may want to give yourself a little holiday between jobs, but that's up to you.

Before You Seriously Start Looking

Before you go out on interviews, get your portfolio organized. Review it and cut out anything that you're not 100 percent proud of. At least 80 percent of your portfolio should be real client work from your first job.

If you still have student work that you want to show—maybe it's in an area that wasn't part of your first job—that's fine, but put it at the back of your presentation. It shouldn't be more than 20 percent of your portfolio.

Don't Make This Mistake with Your Portfolio

Creative people often have a range of interests beyond their work. Graphic designers might also paint in oils, sculpt, or illustrate comic books. Copywriters may be writing fiction or screenplays on the side. These days everyone seems to be a photographer or filmmaker.

If these interests have become part of your professional work— for example, if in addition to your design work on client websites, you've also provided the photography—then, by all means, feature these samples in your portfolio.

But if these are personal interests that have never crossed over to your professional life, you might choose to mention them on your résumé under "Other Interests". I would suggest they have no place in the body of your portfolio.

I still remember a designer coming in to show her portfolio. Most of it was good design work, but at least a third consisted of photos of her oil paintings. They were interesting enough but completely distracting and irrelevant to the job. Stick to samples that show off your professional work.

Should Videographers and Photographers Have Paper Leave-Behinds? Yes

As a videographer and photographer, your work is online. You'll have your website, a YouTube channel, an Instagram account, and likely other social media. That's how you'll present your work.

But when the meeting is over, what do you leave behind so they'll remember you? A two-page résumé? You could be one of dozens of people they see.

I can tell you from the interviewing side, it's hard to keep track:

"Who was that guy we saw the other day with the cool snow-boarding spot?"

"I dunno, I think his résumé is around here somewhere. Did he email the URLs?"

"Not sure. I'll look...."

You don't want to be that guy. You want to be as memorable as possible and easy to contact.

Get a designer friend to put together a portfolio book of screen-grabs, URLs, contact information, and maybe a few words from you on every project. Get some personality in there. Stand out from everyone else. Print it out, leave it behind. Make yourself memorable.

A tip on leave-behind portfolios: have them designed on 11 x 17 paper in landscape orientation, rather than the standard letter size 8 ½ x 11. The larger size makes for an impactful presentation, and most importantly, it's too big for most filing cabinets. There's a good chance it will stay on top of the desk as a constant reminder.

Get Personal Business Cards

Once you're in the business, you'll meet people at various shows, conferences, and industry nights. You'll want to stay in touch with each other.

Yes, you can exchange contact information electronically, but often that means you get added to their contact database. You don't stand out, and you get buried with all the other contacts. It's not very memorable.

For greater impact, you want to hand out a business card. Always ask for a card in return. It might feel old school, but many people will appreciate it.

This should be your personal card. If you're an employee somewhere, you might have a business card from the company. But you should also have your own card, like a calling card.

What goes on the card? Your name, what you do (copywriter, designer, photographer, filmmaker), phone number, email address, and social media addresses. You don't need a street address.

If you're not a designer, get a designer to do it for you, and then choose a quality paper stock (trust me, the paper stock makes all the difference, so don't cheap out here).

You can also go on sites like Fiverr, Upwork, and Etsy to find designers worldwide who will create to your specifications.

Bonus tip: make your business card the standard business card size. No folded cards, no strange sizes. All the essential information goes on one side. You can put a design or graphic on the backside.

I've seen many "creative" business cards, and nine times out of ten, they just feel flakey. Don't do that.

This is the time to be practical, showing both design sense and common sense.

How to Choose Your Second Company

Leaving one job and starting at another can be a very emotional event. It's not something you want to do on a whim. Before making the leap, consider the following:

- Do your research on the prospective employer. Start with their website and social media. How do they portray themselves? Look for examples of recent work on their site.
- After reviewing their site, go further. See whether they've been covered in industry publications or broad media.
- Review their clients. Are these the clients you want to work for?
- See whether they enter and win at awards shows.
- Do you know anyone who works there, currently or recently? Check on LinkedIn or other social media sites. If so, get in touch with them, buy them a coffee, and ask questions.
- If you're not desperate, be fussy in choosing your next job. If you're looking at an agency's site and it doesn't appeal to you, or you're hearing negative things about them, skip it. Take your time. Find an agency that you think will be a great place to work. Don't settle.

If you're answering an ad, you'll want to do as much research as possible in a day or two and then make up your mind whether you want to apply. If so, get your application in early.

You Want to Work at a Company, but They're Not Hiring (Today)

If you answer an ad for a company looking to hire, you should know that they will probably be flooded. You could be one of dozens of applicants. So, make sure your résumé and cover letter stand out. You get one chance to make a first impression. Your response is that chance.

However, you should also consider identifying companies you'd like to work for, whether they're currently advertising to hire or not.

In my agencies, we often hired without running ads. We would ask our staff whether they knew anyone suitable for the position. We would speak to our contacts. If someone had previously sent us an interesting résumé, we might contact that person. Only if none of those avenues worked would we put out an ad.

It's worth getting in touch with companies where you'd like to work, whether or not they're advertising.

First, figure out who to contact and start with a well-written email. Make it personal and specifically for that company. Don't blast out generic emails. Let the recipient know that you've been following their company, enjoy the work they do, and would like to discuss any potential opportunities.

Include a link to your website (you have one, right?) with your résumé and portfolio. Ask for a meeting to get feedback on your work.

In most cases, you will get a response of some kind. If you don't hear back within a week, send a short, polite follow-up email. If you don't hear back after that, drop it. They're not interested enough to reply. Any further attempts at contact just become annoying.

Your goal is to get a meeting where you can present yourself and your work. You'll get a better sense of what they're about, and they'll understand what you do.

They might not be looking today, but they will be someday. You want to "jump the queue" and get to the top of the line. Maybe they'll just call you rather than putting out an ad.

Ideally, for the meeting, you'll have some sort of paper leave-behind piece. You always want to leave a reminder. Put it on tabloid-size paper or in some type of portfolio, container, or book that stands out.

You Got Your Second Job—Now What?

Congratulations, you're working your way up. In your second job, you should do the same things you did in your first job:

- Do great work and continue to build a fantastic portfolio.
- Take note of how the company operates and think about how that compares to your previous place of employment. What can you learn from that?
- Make new contacts to build your network.
- Stay in touch with work friends from your first job.
- Work hard.
- Save money—you'll need it to start your own business.

By your second job, you're into the third to fifth year of your career. At this point, you will likely be involved in client meetings, presenting, and taking feedback. Pay attention to your client interaction skills. Work on your presentations. Learn from the more senior members of your team.

Remember, in addition to your job, you have a "secret job." You're preparing for your agency.

Again, make note of the systems that manage projects and how they communicate and archive files. Consider your job as personal training. One day soon, you'll have to be a master of client management, presentations, and operations.

Look for a Third Job? Maybe

Here's where it gets very personal—you'll have to figure out for yourself whether you want to continue being an employee for a while longer or go out on your own.

There's nothing wrong with being in the business as an employee for 10–15 years or more before starting on your own. That's an individual choice.

But since this book is about starting your own agency, I'm going to assume that sooner or later, you're going to launch your company.

What about Being an Employee Forever?

Let's look at another option. What if you were to stay an employee forever? What if you find a company that you like, with people you get along with, and clients that are interesting and fun? Couldn't you just stay there forever? Maybe, but these days, I don't think it's a great strategy. Here's why.

Let's say you come into this position at an intermediate to senior level, whether you're a writer, designer, film editor, or photographer. For the first few years, you're getting more experience on various projects, and you're noticeably improving at what you do.

Your creative work is on the mark, you're diplomatic with clients and an accomplished presenter in the boardroom. You're a real asset to the business.

Depending on how the company is structured, you may also be given a title and a supervisory role over some juniors. But note, you are not a partner in the company. You are perhaps the most senior employee.

Over the years, you will have received appropriate raises and bonuses. But at about year eight to ten, the situation changes. You're going to hit a wall. The company cannot pay you any more than you're making. Why? Well, simply because you're not worth it.

You've maxed out your salary for that position. At some point, they may even think that for your salary, they would be better off by hiring two intermediates.

Also, what does it say when you've been there for so long, and they haven't offered you any kind of partnership?

The simple answer: likely, the owners are not interested in more partners. Perhaps this is not a reflection on you, but just that they're happy with the current ownership structure and don't want to expand it.

Here's another consideration. If there's a downturn in business (a big client leaves) and the company needs to reduce salaries, yours becomes a prime candidate. By losing just one person, the company has substantially cut back its overhead.

And finally, if you've had a lifer mentality and assumed you would stay there until you retired, you probably haven't developed a freelance business on the side. You've been happy to do your job and not think too far beyond that.

Let's say that for some reason, you decide to, or are forced to, leave at about year fifteen. Now you're out looking for a job. You haven't done that in ages.

Your portfolio may be relatively narrow in scope since all of your recent work has been for the clients of one agency. The people you're interviewing with will wonder why you stayed so long. You'll be asking for a big salary. Hiring someone like you would be a tough decision for any company.

Realistically, I think that once you're in a senior position as an employee, you have to be looking at some kind of ownership, whether it's as a partner in an existing firm or starting your own agency. Otherwise, you limit your income and put your future in jeopardy.

The creative agency business is not a "gold watch after twenty-five years" environment. Keep this in mind and plan ahead. Make sure that you're in control of your career and the decisions you make along the way.

It can be a rude awakening to be living on a high salary for years and then get pushed to the curb. Don't let it happen to you.

Chapter Takeaways

- If you're working for an agency, you have two jobs: the job you were hired to do and learning how the business actually works. That's a free education that will help you start your own company.
- Be in charge of your career. Apply at companies where you want to work. Ignore the opportunities that don't thrill you.
- As you get more experience and seniority, you need to make plans for ownership of some type. Either become a partner in an existing firm or start your own. It may feel risky, but it's the safest option.

5

STARTING YOUR FREELANCE BUSINESS

"It is good to love many things, for therein lies the true strength, and whosoever loves much performs much, and can accomplish much, and what is done in love is well done."

— Vincent Van Gogh

Prepare for Starting Your Own Business with Freelance Clients

Working full-time for someone else can take up your whole day. The creative agency business is notorious for long hours and sudden deadlines that need immediate attention.

You might ask, "How could I possibly do anything else on top of that?" I understand, but now is the time to get some freelance clients to start building your foundation. That means you'll be working on those jobs evenings and weekends.

Two things to keep in mind: first, it's quite common for employees in the creative services business to also do freelance work on the side. As long as your day job comes first, there should be no issues with working freelance.

But just to be sure, if you signed an employment contract, see whether it mentions anything about freelance work.

Second, ethics come into play. You should not work for a client that is a competitor to any clients your current employer has.

When you became an employee, your employment agreement likely included a confidentiality clause stating that all information relating to the company's clients is confidential and not to be shared.

Working in this environment, you'll see client information that is not yet public and could be of value to a competitor.

To provide a simple example, if your employer has a soft drink client, whether or not you work on that account, you can't work freelance for another soft drink company. It's unethical and is a potential conflict of interest that could cost you your job. Although the offer may be tempting, there's only one answer, and that's no.

Get Organized for Your Future Life Now

As you're working freelance, set yourself up for how you're going to work independently. That includes writing detailed estimates for your clients, tracking your time, and billing in an organized fashion.

Consider using a project management solution from the beginning. You want to get into the habit of tracking and monitoring your work. It may seem like overkill when you're working by yourself, but it will help you determine how long it takes you to do the projects and whether your estimates are accurate.

Some of these project management programs also include functionality for creating estimates and invoices. Having this information together in one place will help you keep organized and make it easy to review your progress over time.

Assuming you're doing most of your freelance work from a home office, you'll want to speak to your accountant about claiming some tax deductions against your freelance income.

That could include a percentage of household expenses such as rent, mortgage, and utilities, depending on your office setup. Check to see whether you need a separate office room, not your kitchen table, to be able to claim deductions. It may vary, depending on where you live.

Cultivate a Professional Attitude

The more professionally you present yourself and run your freelance business, the more professionally you'll be treated, which includes getting paid.

By nature, the agency business attracts people with an artistic mindset. We are the ones who create something out of nothing, who take vague ideas through to finished products that influence millions of people.

On one level, we're artists, but at the same time, we're working in a professional capacity, delivering against client briefs and budgets.

In our minds, it can be a balancing act between being an artist and a businessperson. When it comes to dealing with your clients, be a businessperson.

Be reliable and responsible, friendly and relatable. Be helpful and genuinely engaged with your clients' businesses. Go beyond the bare minimum that is expected of you and over-deliver whenever you can. You are their marketing and communications partner, and it's in your best interest that they see positive results from the work you provide.

At the same time, be matter-of-fact with your estimates, billing, and payment terms. You're a businessperson, and business people get paid. Your freelance work is not a hobby or some half-baked notion. You're providing professional services for which you should be paid accordingly.

It's that type of attitude and approach, along with excellent work, of course, that gets you valuable word-of-mouth recommendations and helps grow your business.

How Do You Get Freelance Clients?

This is where your network comes in and why it's essential to keep in touch with people. In the beginning, you'll get most of your business by word of mouth. But it helps if you lay the groundwork for these introductions and recommendations. There are many ways to get started with freelance clients:

- If you know other freelancers you could team up with, have a meeting to discuss. Common teams include writers and designers, videographers, and editors.
- If you know anyone working at a large company with an internal communications department, ask whether they use freelance talent.
- People may come to you and ask for your specific services. These are likely friends, or friends of friends who have businesses that need your services.
- If you're in your second or third job, get in touch with friends from your previous jobs. Let them know that you're looking for freelance work.
- One of your clients may have left their position and

started their own company or gone to a smaller company and may contact you about providing services. That's why you want to establish relationships with clients and keep up with them.

- Once you get your first freelance client, and assuming you were both happy working together, ask whether they know of anyone else who might use your services. Also, ask for a testimonial.
- You can actively look for clients. There are websites such as Fiverr and Upwork where projects are posted, looking for bids. This would be my least favorite recommendation, but I know some people have made it work. Often it boils down to price. Generally, you don't want to compete at that level.

A word of caution: starting a freelance business can take time. You'll end up doing jobs you don't like. You'll underestimate projects and spend much more time on them than you expected.

You'll get people wanting you to work for free. Likely, you'll have some clients who said they would pay you but take forever. You might even get ripped off—the list goes on.

That's why you want to start when you still have a full-time job with a dependable income. There will be lots of "learning experiences." Try not to make the same mistake twice. Develop a radar for potentially nasty clients and avoid them. Trust your instincts.

What Do Clients Value Most in a Creative Supplier?

A few years ago, there was a survey of clients who hired freelance creative talent. They asked these clients what they valued most in their relationships with suppliers. The answers may surprise you. Stop for a moment and take a guess.

I'll bet many of you thought it would be price—how much people charge, the lower, the better, right? Or perhaps talent. It would make sense that clients value talent the most.

Here are the results of the survey: by far, clients valued reliability over anything else. They wanted people they could count on to meet deadlines and other promises.

In fact, reliability was more than twice as important as the next criteria, which was talent. Talent came in second and the combination of reliability and talent outweighed everything else.

Just below talent, in third position, was personality. How much did they like the person? What was it like to work with them? How did the freelancer handle themselves?

Wait, where is price, the rate? That would be next, right? Wrong. After personality, the next most important factor was, believe it or not, hygiene. How professionally did the person present themselves? Clean, tidy, well-dressed, a regular shower or bath?

And very last, at the bottom of the scale, was the rate. It barely made the cut. How could that be?

If you stop and think about it for a minute, it all makes sense. Turn it upside down to change your perspective. Imagine if you offered the best rate, but you were unreliable, not very talented, had a lousy personality, and your hygiene was terrible. Who would want to work with you? Nobody.

When you start freelancing, remember that reliability is everything. Keep your promises, deliver when you said you would. Once more, the order of importance is:

1. Reliability
2. Talent
3. Personality

4. Hygiene
5. Rate

Make a poster of it. Put it up on your wall.

How I Started Freelancing: Keeping Up with My Network, and an Interesting Offer

I was in my mid-30s, working at a smaller agency full-time. It was my fifth agency. They weren't that busy, which wasn't a good sign.

However, I had kept up with my contacts. One was an account manager I'd worked with at a large agency. He had also left that agency to head up another one. After reviewing their staffing, he called me with a proposition.

They couldn't afford to hire me full-time, but how about working there on a contract, half days, at a guaranteed salary? If they needed me for more than half days, I would bill them at an agreed-upon rate, like a freelance project.

I would have my own office and could work out of there doing my freelance projects with their support staff, computer, printers, etc.

That was a sweet deal! It was a very gentle introduction to doing more freelance work. It got even better when one of our regular supplier reps came by and said he was working for a corporate client that had been using a freelance copywriter. They weren't happy with the writer. Could he put my name forward? Sure...

That one introduction led me to enough freelance business so that I left my half-day arrangement and worked out of my home office full time for the next six years.

Within that first corporate client, I provided services to numerous departments. Also, I had other clients that I met through introductions and recommendations. I then teamed up with other freelancers to provide even more services.

I realized that to grow any further, I needed a different structure than to continue working on my own with other freelancers.

I decided to find a partner to start a larger agency, Fireworks Creative. Five years later, we sold that agency, and I started another one, from which I retired after 15 years.

And that first freelance client? We were still working together 20 years later, after millions of dollars in billing and through numerous corporate and personnel changes. It's all about making and keeping relationships!

A Steady Half-Time Gig Plus Freelancing—Would That Work for You?

My start in freelancing was perfect for me. It was like I had half a job, and it was up to me to fill the other half. Here's the critical part: I didn't look for a second half-day job at another agency.

Having two half-day jobs does not help you start your own business. Yes, it seems more secure, but none of those agency clients will ever be your clients, and they're not helping you build your business.

Take advantage of having someone guarantee you half of every day to build out your client base for the other half.

For a longer-term business, you should start relationships with clients directly, not working as a sub-contractor to agencies. Then one day, make the transition to working solely for yourself.

Caution: Do Not Try to Steal Clients from Someone Who Hired You

If you're working for a company, half-day or full time, you're working on their behalf for their clients. Although you may develop personal relationships with some clients, they don't "belong" to you. They are agency clients.

Your freelance work should be completely separate from your agency work. Even if one of the agency clients takes you aside and suggests that since they like working with you, how about you just work directly with them or do a few projects outside of the agency, the answer is a polite but firm no.

It is unethical, and you could lose your job or get sued. You may have signed an employment agreement that covers this situation, but even if you haven't, it's still unethical. If you get that question, tell them that you're flattered they asked you, but all of your work for them must go through the agency.

However, if your relationship with the agency ends, you are free to work with a client from that previous agency unless there is something specific in your contract to prevent that. Clients can choose to work with whoever they want, and if you would like to work for this client, take it. I wouldn't pursue these clients, but if they call you, it's fair game.

Chapter Takeaways

- Build your network now. That's your future.
- Start freelancing when you have a full-time job. It's the perfect test for running your own company.
- Remember that clients value reliability above all else. You don't want to compete on price for every job. You're not Walmart.

- Consider looking for a half-day job. You could be a great asset for a small- or medium-sized agency. They get an experienced professional but just pay for half the time, with the option of paying by the hour for more time. It's a win-win. You get the rest of the time to start your own business.

6

PREPARING TO LAUNCH YOUR COMPANY

"If you wrote something for which someone sent you a check, if you cashed the check and it didn't bounce, and if you then paid the light bill with the money, I consider you talented."

— Stephen King

Self-Assessment Time: Are You Good Enough to Compete?

Have you ever met someone who has huge dreams, but it's evident to you they don't have the skills to make those dreams a reality? They seem focused on a fantasy of being rich, famous, and admired, only they lack the talent to get there.

Or have you met someone who is reasonably talented at what they do but has zero people skills? In personal interactions, they clam up, mumble, and look at their shoes. They're better off working in the backroom, far away from any client contact.

Some people are very talented in their craft, are excellent employees, and are friendly and personable, but would have no patience for the many other organizational skills it takes to run a company. In other words, great designer but should never be a business owner.

Owning and operating a creative agency of any size means you're going to be wearing many hats, at least at the beginning and perhaps forever. Depending on how many people you'll have in your company, at some point, you'll have to do virtually everything in addition to your core competency.

You'll need to excel at your craft, be personable with clients and employees and be willing to learn the organizational skills you need to manage the business. Ask yourself whether that's you today or could become you in the future.

Excellent at Your Craft, Adequate at Everything Else

The first question you have to think about is whether you have the talent to earn a living at your craft. This is vitally important and is probably the most straightforward question to answer.

If someone has hired you to practice your craft, or you've built up at least a modest freelance practice with repeat clients, then you have the proof that you're good enough.

The only situation where I think you have to question yourself about your craft is if you're coming out of school with the notion of immediately starting your agency.

In most cases, I recommend that if you're a recent graduate, you get a job first to prove to yourself that you can work to professional standards. This also allows you to observe how companies operate.

The more challenging questions you have to ask yourself are about running the business. Broadly, there are two critical aspects to business operations: first, looking outward and working with clients, and second, focusing inward on managing and collaborating with your employees.

Let's address working with clients. Aside from delivering what you're actually doing for them, the other essential parts of the job are the soft "people skills."

How good are you at interacting with others? Can you carry a conversation? Can you take instructions? How do you deal with feedback or criticism of your work? How are your public speaking capabilities? Are you able to address a boardroom where all eyes and ears are on you?

You have to be able to sell your work with confidence, answer questions that sometimes seem to come out of nowhere, and make everyone there thrilled by the fact that you're the one bringing them the innovative solutions.

It's these interpersonal skills that are nearly as important as your actual craft. It comes down to whether clients enjoy being around you. Will they look forward to seeing you? Will they recommend you to others? Do they see you as part of their network?

Keep in mind that, in general, clients aren't bound to you by contract—they can usually change suppliers at any time. There's a saying in the business: "You're only as good as your last job." Part of that job is being someone your client wants to work with again and again.

What are these qualities that make you likable? Mostly it comes down to attention and empathy. When your client speaks, are you listening? Are you genuinely interested in what they say, whether it's about business or their personal life? Or are you just waiting to jump in and talk?

Here's a little test. One of my most important clients had a small dog that she loved very much. As we were getting together for a meeting, she mentioned that her dog was ill and was at the vet.

How would you respond to that? It would be easy to say, "Oh, that's too bad, I hope your dog gets better soon," and then move on to the business at hand. Wrong answer!

I knew how much this dog meant to her, so I kept the conversation going, asking what was wrong, what the vet said, how the dog was the last time she saw it, and so on. She liked talking about her companion. It made her feel better that another person also cared about her dog. Business could wait for a few minutes.

For me, this is not fake empathy. I truly cared about my client, and if she was concerned about her pet, then I wanted to help her feel better.

Another quick story. A different client worked in an office where they had a coffee machine. Unfortunately, the coffee was awful. On my way to meetings with her, I passed by an excellent coffee shop. I would bring her a cup, and one for myself, too. It was a little thing, but she appreciated it. And now, over our meeting, we were drinking coffee together. It brought us closer.

It's these small touches that create strong relationships. It may feel counter-intuitive, but that's what makes the difference. People like to feel special. You should be the one to make them feel that way.

Look for ways to get nearer to your clients in an authentic way. You'll do that by listening and paying attention.

Finally, look at what it would take to manage others in your company, assuming you'll have employees. Imagine yourself as the boss. How will you interact with your employees?

How will you guide and steer them to make sure they turn out work that you can sell to the client, without doing the work for them or antagonizing them with an overbearing attitude?

Keep in mind that talented employees can find other jobs. It's not just about the money for them—if they don't look forward to coming in to work or getting on the conference call with you, they'll soon be looking for their next opportunity.

I know it's hard to answer these types of questions in advance if you've never done it, but try to do a serious self-evaluation. These are all skills you can learn over time.

It's worth remembering that you don't have to be an expert at everything. As your company grows, you'll want to hire people who have skills that are better than yours in particular areas.

For example, once you have one or more project managers on staff, it will be their job to manage the time of other employees. Not to say you won't be involved in that area, but it will be the project manager who works closely with the employees day-to-day.

If you have the opportunity, it's worth talking to friends, colleagues, or other people who already run their own businesses about the various aspects of business operations.

If you already know you need help in certain areas—say making boardroom presentations—consider taking courses now to improve those skills.

Create a Vision for Your Company

It's essential to have a vision for your company before you start. What type of company do you have in mind? Is it full-time? Just you, working as a solopreneur? A few people or many people? Will it be a loose, flexible group or a tight group of integrated specialists?

Will your ideal clients be small businesses, large companies, government, or a combination? Will you specialize in a vertical market, say food and beverage, or will you orient your company around specific deliverables, for example, focusing just on email campaigns?

How do you create a vision for the kind of company you want to build?

The most straightforward place to start is writing down your ideas for what you want your company to be. The vision you come up with should help you and others make decisions that align with your philosophy and goals. You must get the ideas out of your head, so they don't keep spinning round and round.

Once you've written them down, you can review them. Whether it's a journal or a text document, do whatever works for you. That allows you to edit and rearrange your ideas so that the document becomes a good record of your thoughts at the time of writing.

Then sit with it. Live with it for a while. Read about how other companies created their visions and what they are. Read Inc.com and FastCompany.com. Both have lots of information about start-ups of all types and sizes.

If you have someone you can trust to share the idea with, do so. Get some feedback, but don't let anyone change your concept too much.

If you know someone who has started a company within the last few years, buy them a coffee or a beer and pick their brains. I've found that most business owners will gladly talk about their experiences, offering tips and advice.

Keep in mind that you may start with one vision and change it as your business develops. Don't worry about getting it 100 percent right. Once you get closer to starting your company, your ideas will likely shift. That's fine. This first brainstorm will give you a starting point.

A personal note: when my first partner and I started Fireworks Creative, we rented a space designed for seven people. For a while, we sublet some of the workstations. Within a year, we had filled the space. Within four years, we had expanded twice to accommodate 30 people.

We didn't predict that growth rate, but even at the outset, we knew it wasn't going to be just the two of us. Our vision from the beginning was to have a bigger agency serving corporate clients.

Would It Be Easiest to Be a Solopreneur?

Some people know they just want to work on their own on a free-lance basis. They don't want to be bothered with managing or dealing with staff. They're best left alone to focus on their tasks.

There are many very successful single-person companies. Think of writers, illustrators, photographers, editors, and programmers. They may sub-contract others to help on projects, but most of the time, they're working solo.

It's a popular model for those wanting a "digital entrepreneur, global traveler" life. Self-contained, with a laptop and a bit of equipment, working wherever there's an Internet connection. Free to travel, explore the world.

Solopreneurs may work on their own projects or act as suppliers to someone else's projects. This model also works for those who just want to work part-time and have other interests or obliga-tions that take up the rest of their time. It's the most flexible model but also the one requiring the most discipline if it's to be the sole source of income.

The other downside is that as a solopreneur, you're limited by yourself, both in the knowledge you have and the number of hours you have to dedicate to your clients.

You may have so many projects that you're working every hour you're awake. Great for billing (you hope), but lousy for family or social life. Or, you're not very busy and don't know how to generate new business. You had better learn quickly.

Many people also find themselves getting lonely working on their own. Sure, you'll be communicating with clients, but you have no one to brainstorm with and get a second opinion. You have to know yourself to determine whether working solo is for you.

If you're starting solo or plan to continue working that way, you should think about building your network of creative service suppliers so you can team up to deliver whole projects.

For example, if you're a designer, I think you should have a few go-to copywriters, front-end programmers, photographers, and videographers.

You want to be confident that if a client talks to you about a project requiring these services, you can easily say yes, knowing that you have at least a few people at hand who have the skills the project needs. It's better for you to pick your team than have the client hook you up with someone you don't know.

When you talk to people you want to work with, have a few discussions with them to determine how they work, their billing rates, and anything else that might be applicable. Ideally, try working together on a small project before committing to working with them on a larger job.

A Small Company in a Small Town May Be the Answer

Big city life isn't for everyone. If you live in a smaller town, you can establish yourself there. With just a few people, you could find enough business in your region to keep everyone busy.

You don't need to be a big firm with all the challenges and over-head of managing partners and employees. These firms tend to be generalists to take care of the many needs of clients in their markets.

Or, a small-town firm might be highly specialized and be recog-nized for its services in major markets. You can live in Smalltown, Anywhere and still do work for companies in Toronto, New York, Los Angeles, London, or Paris. It just depends on your type of services.

As soon as you think of having an agency that's more than just you, you have to decide whether you're hiring employees, working with contractors, finding a partner, or any combination thereof. But make sure you're only building your company as your billing supports it. Business growth should drive your expansion.

Is This the Sweet Spot—A Medium-Sized Company in a City?

This is what I did with the agencies I launched. Since I live in Toronto, a city of about three million and the largest city in Canada, that's where I established the businesses.

With my advertising agency background working for large corpo-rations and government, I was comfortable in that environment and wanted those types of clients.

They have budgets they need to spend, and for the most part, talented people in their communications and marketing depart-ments who would be our clients.

The benefit of establishing yourself in a large city is that there is potential business all around you, along with deep pools of talent to staff your company. At the same time, keep in mind that you're surrounded by significant competition. So, you have to earn your business.

If your vision is to have employees working out of your office, you'll have a higher monthly overhead. Big-city rent is expensive. Add to that the cost of benefits beyond salary, parking, and various taxes.

You'll have to determine the right size and combination of talent to serve your clients, knowing that you can also draw on freelance or contract talent as needed. A medium-sized company would have 10–50 employees. Above that, you're a larger company that requires additional management capabilities.

How About a Small Nucleus Augmented by Freelancers?

Today, many entrepreneurs are starting companies based on having a few people at the core, augmented by a select group of freelancers and contractors. The core group may work out of an office or out of their homes.

There are a few critical aspects to making this work. The first is to find freelancers who can consistently deliver to your expectations at rates that you can mark up so that it's profitable for you. Just as importantly, you'll need strong project management to ensure everyone works together smoothly, hitting critical deadlines and delivering as expected.

Working with freelancers, you have to be prepared for the fact that they may not be available when you need them, and you'll need an alternate for that project.

Lastly, you'll want to develop policies that your freelancers agree to before working together. At the very least, the guidelines will address expectations, payment terms, and client ownership.

This working style is becoming more common as many people have become accustomed to working and communicating remotely. It takes more management skills but can reduce monthly costs significantly.

National or Global Company

Although many large companies start small and grow to national or international size, others are planned that way from the outset. They're often founded by a group of people who leave a larger firm to start their own. From the first day, they plan to be a big company.

In the creative services field, this has often been accomplished by having a core company and then acquiring other specialty companies to augment their services. It's been a successful model for those with the management skills and ability to attract financing to fund the growth.

For this book, we're going to ignore this group. This is the least likely option for a new company, and I assume those who are planning to go this route know everything they need to launch and succeed.

When Will You Know You're Ready to Launch?

Knowing when you're ready to launch is a very individual decision. If you've had the security of a steady job where you could count on getting paid regularly, cutting the cord and making the leap to independence can be frightening.

Here is what I think you need to make that decision:

- You should have a substantial and consistent freelance business that you can transition to your new company. If you're lucky, one or two of your freelance clients will have much more work for you now that you're creating a bigger agency.

- Having a partner or spouse with a steady income will certainly help. Could you live off that one income for a time if you had to?
- A tough one: try to ensure that the rest of your life—your family, relationships, and health—are in order. If your personal life is a major distraction, it will be challenging to focus on building your new business.

You Saved Some Money to Start Your Business, Right?

Before you get too far down the road in launching your new business, make sure you're financially ready. Depending on what you have in mind, you will likely need a cushion to tide you over your initial launch.

Most people recommend three months' living expenses in the bank. A past employee of mine was more conservative—he didn't launch his own company until he had six months saved up.

I was lucky. In my situation, I had a steady part-time income, and as my freelance income increased, I gave up my part-time income and made the transition to full-time freelance.

At the time, I had also saved some money, knowing that there could be periods when I wouldn't be busy and have very little in receivables. I was also working from home and already had a home office, so there was no added expense. And—can't forget this—my wife had a good income, so that I was not the only one working in our household.

Do a realistic evaluation of your situation. Being completely broke is no way to start a business.

Having significant monthly expenses such as rent, car payments, student debt, and credit card debts will also rob you of your confidence. You'll be tempted to take on any project, even those that aren't right for you, because you're desperate for the money.

You'll have enough to think about in the early days of your business without worrying about crushing debt.

Key considerations: are you working from home, or will you need an office? If you're working from home and assuming you have the equipment you need, you'll have minimal overhead expenses.

On the other hand, if it's an office, is it a shared space where you can pay by the month with no additional expenses, or are you signing a lease on a space where you'll need to pay first and last month's rent, buy furniture, and perhaps pay to make some renovations?

You should be confident that you are financially set to make it through your company's early months. Do a quick calculation of your monthly expenses versus the money at hand to determine whether you're ready to launch.

Be Very Careful of the "Financed My Business on Credit Cards" Stories

We've all read the articles of two guys in a garage starting their new business by having a dozen credit cards each, until one day their venture took off, and now they're gazillionaires. These are exciting stories and look good on websites for entrepreneurs.

But for every success in this genre, there are hundreds of stories that nobody wants to tell you. Stories of losing everything and declaring personal bankruptcy because they didn't have a plan or the plan they had just didn't work out. That's the more common version. Don't be that story.

If you don't have enough personal capital to finance your start-up, you have a few other options. You could wait until you have saved enough to start. Perhaps "family and friends" will help finance you at favorable rates.

Do you have a house that you can take out a mortgage on? Can you get a personal line of credit with much more reasonable interest rates? If you go the line of credit route, just remember that it is a demand loan, and the bank can call it at any time.

Any of these loans, whether from friends and family, mortgage, or line of credit, carry risk. To some degree, you are always at the whim of the lender.

What if your "family and friends" decide they need their money back sooner than you'd agreed? Or the bank demands you clear up your line of credit?

And to state the obvious, these are loans that you need to pay back regularly, so remember to include that in your budgets.

Ideally, you should be self-funded. But whatever you do, stay away from consumer credit cards and their usurious interest rates. It's no way to finance a start-up. Make sure you have a real financial plan. If you don't, you are not ready to start.

Chapter Takeaways

- Check where you are in your career to ensure you're good enough to compete against others. When you're prospecting, potential clients will want to see your portfolio as proof. Is it good enough to get the clients you want?
- How are your interpersonal skills? You want clients that stick with you for the long term, and a big part of that is to be likable and empathetic. For some, this comes naturally. If not, you need to practice.
- Think hard about the structure of the company you want

to launch. Each is unique and requires different skills. Write out the vision for your company with as many details as possible.

- If your plan is to work solo, do you have a team of freelancers you can count on to augment your skills so that you can deliver complete projects?
- Do you have a base of freelance clients? If not, work on that before launching. These will be the first clients of your new agency. It's imperative that you launch with clients.
- Do a thorough review of your finances. Be realistic. It should be money in the bank that you can easily access. Don't brush this off. Make a detailed plan on paper. Do the math on your monthly expenses. Once you launch, there's no easy way of going back. You need three to six months in the bank.
- Stay away from financing your business on credit cards.

7

BUSINESS STRUCTURES—WHICH ONE IS RIGHT FOR YOU?

"I thrive in structure. I drown in chaos."

— Anna Kendrick

Basic Guide to Business Structures

Please note that these business structures refer to the U.S. and Canada.

Allowable business structures vary by country, state, province, and region. For any structure that you're considering, you'll want to account for the impact on your taxes, liability, and the cost of setting up and maintaining the company.

Talk to your accountant first. (See the section on why getting the right accountant is so vital when you start your business.) Although accountants can't offer you legal advice, they should have experience working with most of these company structures. That will give you an idea of what's most appropriate for you, which you can then confirm in a short meeting with a lawyer.

5

Fundamentally, there are three options for setting up your own business. You can work as an individual, as a member of a partnership, or as an employee of your own incorporated company.

There may be a few choices within those structures, such as Limited Liability Partnerships, depending on where you live. In the creative services field, the most popular options are sole proprietor and incorporated company.

Working as an Individual—A Sole Proprietor

Many people start as a sole proprietor, generally because it's faster and cheaper. Later they often migrate to another structure.

Let's look at what it means to be a sole proprietor:

- At a basic level, you and your business are one and the same.
- Your income gets taxed as personal income.
- For tax purposes, you can deduct expenses from this income. That includes everything related to you making money, including the cost of equipment, office space, business travel, entertaining clients, etc. You need to keep receipts for everything so your accountant can do your taxes.
- Be careful with writing off expenses, and make sure they're legitimate. Government tax departments pay close attention to expense claims.
- You can hire people by the project, on contract, or full-time. However, as an employer, you're responsible for all employment administration and recordkeeping, especially concerning withholding taxes and contributions to the taxes for any full-time employee. If you're hiring employees, check with your accountant to ensure you get this right.

- You can hire your spouse, partner, or children, as long as they perform legitimate work for you. If you hire them by the job or on contract, you need invoices from them. If they are employees, you need to treat them like employees from a taxation perspective. Don't fall into the trap of setting up a casual financial relationship where you think you can simply give them random amounts of money periodically. You'll have significant tax issues.
- You can give your company a name other than your name. However, you'll need to open a separate bank account if you're getting paid under the company name.

Critical Disadvantages for Sole Proprietors

There are two significant disadvantages to being a sole proprietor.

First, as a sole proprietor operating an unincorporated business, you are personally liable for everything related to your business. There is no separation between you and your company—you are your business, and your business is you. Generally, this lack of separation doesn't matter.

However, if something goes dramatically wrong and someone sues you, they can go after everything you personally own—your house, car, savings, your awesome vinyl collection, everything.

Second, and much more importantly, from a taxation perspective, all income is taxed as your personal income. That means you may end up paying more in taxes than if you were incorporated. At the very least, you have far less flexibility in tax planning.

As an example, let's say you have an income of $100,000. Let's assume $20,000 in expenses. That leaves $80,000 to be taxed at personal tax levels. You can't "leave money in the company" that won't get taxed at personal rates because you are the company.

However, to offset that and assuming you don't need the money, you can open an Individual Retirement Account (IRA) in the U.S. or a Registered Retirement Savings Plan (RRSP) in Canada to reduce your taxable income.

If you're just starting and you want to save money, there's nothing wrong with working as a sole proprietor for a while. Once your business grows, I would recommend that you incorporate.

Keep in mind that if you make this change, you'll have to inform your clients of your new name, structure and banking information.

For myself, I incorporated all of my companies right at the beginning. I didn't see any sense in working one way for a while and then switching. But, your mileage may vary, so speak to your accountant to determine what's right for you.

You Can Also Have a Partnership

If you have business partners, you can set up a formal partnership. The terms of the partnership will be in your agreement. Note that although this is a legal structure, it has no impact on your taxes. You will still be taxed personally on any income derived from the partnership. You can have either a Limited Liability Company or Limited Liability Partnership.

What are LLCs or LLPs?

Limited Liability Companies (LLC) or Limited Liability Partnerships (LLP) are structures that are available in some states and provinces. Specific laws vary, so if you're interested, you'll need a legal opinion for your region.

Both structures are set up to protect you from liability. However, in most cases, they have no impact on taxes. Taxes are not paid by

LLCs or LLPs, but by the individuals, so in that way, they're similar to being a Sole Proprietor or a Partner. In my experience, I haven't seen these structures being popular in the creative agency field.

Working in an Incorporated Structure

Even if you're working solo, you may want to incorporate. By doing so, you become an employee of your own company. You will file both a corporate tax return and a personal return. You might choose this route right from the beginning.

Corporate tax rates are generally lower than personal rates. With a corporation, you have much more flexibility in how and when you pay yourself for tax planning purposes. There is a clear distinction between company money and your personal money.

For example, you can pay yourself a modest salary and then pay yourself a dividend in the next tax year.

So, assuming your company billed $100,000 and had $20,000 in expenses, from the remaining $80,000, you could choose to pay yourself $60,000 and leave the other $20,000 in the company to add to your cushion. (You always want money in the bank because your business and receivables will vary from month to month.)

Then, at a later date, perhaps in the following year, sit down with your accountant and declare a dividend to yourself. It could be the $20,000 you left in the bank, or more or less, depending on your finances.

You'll still pay taxes on that dividend, but you've pushed it out a year, and tax rates on dividends are lower than salary. In the meantime, your company might be able to pay you enough so you can put away some funds into an IRA or RRSP to defer personal taxes.

With a corporation, you can limit any potential liability to your company and protect yourself personally. Most contracts you sign are only on behalf of your company.

However, be ready for some people, especially landlords, to make you sign personally as well. There's not much you can do to avoid that if you want to sign the lease. But in general, demands for personal guarantees are rare.

Also, an incorporated company looks and feels more significant and more formal to clients and anyone else you might work with —"Smith Design Inc." carries more weight than "Bob Smith, Designer."

In the same vein, larger clients are more comfortable dealing with incorporated companies. In some cases, they may insist on proof of your incorporation and further evidence that you carry certain levels of liability insurance.

Take Care of Legal Requirements for an Incorporated Business Early

If you decide to have an incorporated business, you have to file for incorporation in your area. Every jurisdiction has its specific requirements for recognizing businesses for legal and taxation purposes.

Speak to your accountant or lawyer, or simply search incorporating a business in [the name of your state or province] and look for the official site.

Many licensed incorporation agents can handle the incorporation for you, including the name search, filing your papers, getting a business number, and giving you all your necessary documentation. You'll see these companies when you do your search.

Fees vary by jurisdiction, from about $250 to $1,500. I was surprised by the range, having only incorporated companies in Ontario.

You'll need your incorporation paperwork and your business number to open a bank account for the business and, in some cases, to enter into contracts with clients. Generally, you should have everything from your agent within a week or so, but check ahead if you're in a hurry.

What Should Your Company's Legal Name Be?

If you haven't settled on a name for your company, you can still register your business as a numbered company. Then you'll be something like 1234567 Ontario o/a (operating as) [Name of Company] until you have the name, though you can also leave the numbered name.

In my companies, people knew us by our company names. As legal structures, we were numbered companies. You only have to use the numbered company name on legal documents. You don't need it on your communications materials.

Your clients can make out their checks or deposits to your company name. They don't need to know your company number.

A Few Words on Naming Your Company

There are many books and articles written on naming companies or products. It's probably worth reading some if you're looking for a name. But, here is a summary of my thoughts:

- You could use your name as a corporate name, but it gets problematic if you take on partners. It will always seem like just your company, and they may feel like they're riding second class. If you have Bob Smith Design Inc. as a name, and John Brooks is your partner, John may feel left out. But there are plenty of big agencies named after founders, e.g., J. Walter Thompson, Ogilvy & Mather, so you'll have to decide whether this works for you.

- Ideally, your company name should be easy to say and spell. If you use a hard-to-spell name, you'll always be spelling it out. Also, if it's too quirky, it may feel flakey, but that's your call.
- Two things you need to check: first, can you legally use that name? Generally, a name search is part of the service provided by your incorporation agent. They do a Newly Updated Automated Name Search (NUANS) to ensure another company isn't using the name in your jurisdiction.
- Second, can you get a URL for that name or a close variation of it? Be diligent on this. You don't want to settle on a name, start your business, and then find out you can't get a good URL.
- Your first choice for a URL should be a .com, but if they're all taken, you can try for one of the other domain suffixes, such as .co, .io, and .net.
- If you want a URL that someone else registered but isn't using, you might want to pursue buying it. Sometimes you'll get a ridiculous price of hundreds of thousands of dollars, but you may be surprised.
- Once, I was looking for a name that was taken but not being used. I contacted the owner. He said he had registered it for a project that didn't work out, and that he was going to let the registration expire the next month. Great timing. I grabbed it the day it expired. Nice guy—thank you!

Chapter Takeaways

- If you start the business on your own, you can begin by working as a sole proprietor in an unincorporated structure. As your business grows, you could then make a change to a different structure.
- Speak to your accountant because your business structure will have an impact on your taxes.
- Before you finalize your company structure, you may want to get legal advice since the laws for corporations can vary by state, province, or district.
- In my case, I incorporated my companies right at the outset under my provincial jurisdiction.
- Choose a name that will work for you long term.

8

WRITING A BUSINESS PLAN

"Plans are worthless, but planning is everything."

— U.S. President Dwight D. Eisenhower

Writing a Business Plan—Should You Do It?

Writing a detailed business plan for your new agency could take you weeks, maybe months. So, should you do it? There are solid arguments for writing one. Every business book will tell you to do it.

On the other hand, the renegades will say that anything more than a page or two is a waste of time since there's so much speculation involved.

I'll side with the traditionalists. I think you should write a short business plan, even if it's just as an exercise to force you to think about aspects of running a business that you hadn't considered. It's your opportunity to get all those thoughts out of your head and onto paper in an organized fashion.

Another way of looking at a business plan is that it's a formalized structure for setting goals. What client sectors are you going to target so that you'll meet your financial goals?

This will lead you to think about the types of activities you'll have to undertake to get in front of those clients. If you think you're going to self-finance your company, your business plan is a way of creating a blueprint for yourself with some markers to see how you're doing.

On the other hand, if you're looking for financing, whether it's friends and family or outside sources, you'll definitely need a business plan. They'll want to know how you're going to run the company, and most importantly, how you're going to pay them back.

Your plan is your credibility on paper. Potential lenders will judge your prospects for success by what they know of you and what you've included in your documentation. Is your plan realistic? Is it comprehensive? Have you come up with believable numbers and timelines? Are you the person to put this plan into action?

Business Plan Templates

A simple online search will bring you lots of information about writing a business plan and templates ranging from the very simple to the incredibly detailed. There are also dozens of books on the subject.

It's worth spending time evaluating the various resources to determine how you want to structure your plan. A template for a simple business plan looks something like this:

Vision: A vision that outlines your hopes and dreams for your company. What type of company is it? How will it start up? Where do you see it in three to five years? Will the company focus on a specialty area? If so, provide support for why this will be a successful approach.

Business Objective: Your business objective will describe how you'll achieve your vision. It should include a description of your target market (spell out the size and industries for your ideal clients), a list of services you'll provide, why they'll buy from you (what are your selling propositions), and how you'll deliver those services.

You might also want to include information about your competitors in the field and why you think you'll be successful against them.

Financial Strategy: In summary, this section should demonstrate how you'll make your business profitable. What are your projected revenues and expenses? How will you charge? What makes you competitive in your market? What proof do you have that your financial strategy is realistic, not just tables of made-up numbers?

Advertising and Promotion: How will you promote your business? Typically, it would include at least some of the following: a website, social media, advertising, referrals, PR, public speaking, and trade shows. Who is going to do this?

Timeline: What do you hope to achieve by significant milestones: first six months, first year, second year. You can state this in many ways: how much revenue, how many clients, how profitable, how much you get paid, number of staff, etc.

Action Calendar: To meet your objectives, you will have to complete a long list of tasks. Break down your goals as a "to do" list and put dates next to when you will complete each task.

Get Feedback on Your Plan

Before you show your business plan to anyone who might lend you money, it's a good idea to invite feedback. Even if you're not looking for outside capital, you should seek an objective opinion on your plan.

If you have an accountant, they would be a natural person to ask for a review. If you have friends or colleagues who are already in the creative agency business or friends in banking or lending who have reviewed business plans, ask them.

You're looking for questions that will help you clarify your thinking, uncover false assumptions, add missing information, and hone your plan.

Personal Experience with Business Plans

I've written or co-written a few business plans. Here's what I found valuable in the exercise:

1. The plans acted as a way of consolidating my thoughts at a point in time. They helped me weed out directions that sounded interesting, but on closer inspection, were unrealistic.
2. The plans forced me to think about the types of clients I wanted to attract and how I would go about attracting them. On the other side of the coin, they made me think about the types of clients I didn't want and why I didn't want them.
3. The plans acted as "to do" lists that I could check off as I accomplished the tasks. It's always a good feeling to check things off a list.
4. The plans were also a wake-up call on the expense side, realizing I would have to pay for any grandiose visions.

When I reviewed the plans, it was interesting to see how the fore-casts turned out. Some of the numbers were substantially off. In my first company, we hired too fast as the company grew, and our payroll was out of proportion against our revenue.

On the other hand, clients led us into business areas we hadn't anticipated, which turned out very well. We had a marketing person who had a unique way of finding projects that were substantially larger than we had imagined, which dramatically increased our profile and allowed us to tackle even bigger projects.

In general, I wouldn't attempt to create forecasts for more than three years, and realistically, the first year of any plan is the most important.

At the end of the 12 months, you'll have year-end numbers from your accountant, which you can plug into your plan as a basis for going forward.

It's always a good reality check to compare your first-year numbers to your projections. How realistic was your thinking? How does that affect your plans? Year ends are always a time of reckoning.

Add This to your Business Plan: Brainstorm a Prospect List

In addition to your business plan, and for internal use only (no need to share this), elaborate on the Business Objective of your plan by creating a prospect list.

This list should be any company, organization, or government department that you'd like as a client. Don't hold back. For now, don't worry about how realistic the list will be, but only include those for whom you'd like to work.

Your list should be well over 100 names. Don't stop until you're into three digits. You might have to do some research to identify companies you didn't know about, but upon consideration, you'd like to work for them.

Why do this? It's to open up your thinking about who you might want to work for. You'll have companies and organizations on that list that you previously hadn't contemplated. One company will lead to another.

Now think about anyone you might know in any of those companies. Look at LinkedIn and social media to start making connections.

These can become your prime prospects for reaching out, letting them know what you're doing. They should be soft outreaches, not attempts at hard pitches. For now, you just want to get on their radar.

Before You Get Too Far, Find a Good Accountant

I was lucky. When I started freelancing, one of my colleagues gave me the name of an accountant with many clients in the creative agency business (along with a few very famous authors, hello Margaret Atwood and Michael Ondaatje!). Up until then, I had been doing my taxes.

Why was the accountant so critical? When you're starting a business, no matter how you want to structure it, there are so many things you just don't know. You need someone you can talk to about finances and running your business.

Ideally, you want an accountant who has clients similar to you and the business you're starting. Your accountant should understand your business and its challenges.

In my case, he outlined how other companies like ours ran their business (in general, without sharing confidential information). He gave me profitability projections and various financial ratios (gross billing/overhead/profit). His insights helped me create targets to aim for in my operations.

Your accountant can also make suggestions for specific book-keeping and project management software. In short, your accountant can be your business sounding board through various stages of your growth.

Find someone who can help you in a consulting and advisory capacity, rather than just doing your taxes once a year. You need to feel comfortable enough with them to discuss everything about your business. After all, they are going to know about every dollar of your business and life.

If you don't get that kind of advice or comfort from your current accountant, find another one as soon as possible. Don't delay. Used properly, your accountant can be your best advisor, and at the early stages of your business life, you likely need as much help as you can get.

How do you find such a person? Ask around. Talk to other company owners. Get in touch with your local graphic design or marketing association and ask them for referrals.

I found my current accountant because he was a speaker at a creative services conference (public speaking was his way of finding new clients in this sector—it worked). He has many clients in the creative services field, which enables him to offer highly relevant advice and insight.

Before you choose an accountant, you may want to ask how they charge. Like other professional service advisors, their fees will vary. Some may bundle services, while others charge by the hour.

For me, I was guided by the fact that my accountant had other clients like me. I assumed his fees were reasonable for the services provided, and I was happy with them. But, it doesn't hurt to ask—after all, your clients ask you about your fees.

Your Accountant Should Make You Financially Literate

In addition to taking care of your taxes and providing advice, you want your accountant to help you become financially literate when it comes to running your company.

Assuming this is your first company, and you've never reviewed the typical financial statements that every company produces, it might seem complicated, and if you're not a numbers person, incredibly dull.

Your job is to get a grasp of at least the most critical numbers in these documents, to know with greater certainty that you're doing well. You should be able to look at a few key indicators to see whether or not you're on the right path to hitting your targets.

Your accountant's job is to explain this to you in a way that you'll understand. The accountant can also give you guidance for specific benchmarks that you should be achieving and advice on how to correct course if you're not hitting them.

There are three documents you should review regularly. Keep in mind that these documents show history, what happened over a defined period. But soon, you'll see patterns that will help you predict the financial future of your company. Once you have a basic understanding of what these documents tell you, you'll want to review them monthly.

The first document is your Income Statement (aka Profit and Loss, or P&L). Your income statement can be for any period you choose—just pick the start and end dates, and your accounting software does the rest.

Typically, you'd look at monthly, quarterly, and annual statements. The Income Statement focuses on four essential items: your revenue, expenses, gains, and losses. It includes the details of your sales and then works down to your net income. It tells you how much money you took in, what happened to it and how that compares to the previous period.

Next comes the Balance Sheet. A Balance Sheet is a snapshot representing your company's finances at a moment in time. It lists your assets, liabilities, and shareholders' equity, basically showing you what you own and what you owe on that date.

You can think of your Balance Sheet as a summary of the detail shown in your Income Statement.

Any single Balance Sheet won't give you a sense of trends in your company's finances, but reviewing a series of Balance Sheets, say, one for every month, will start to show you what's happening in your company. This is, in fact, the best indicator of how your company is doing.

The last financial document to review is your Cash Flow Statement.

The Cash Flow Statement is also for a defined period (month, quarter, year). It includes four critical pieces of information. It tells you how much cash there was at the beginning of the statement, how much came in during the defined period, how much went out, and how much is left.

Once you're up and running for six months or so, it will be instructive to compare your financial results to your business plan. How are you doing compared to what you thought when you wrote the business plan?

It can be a sobering reality check and may cause you to make some changes. You may want to update your business plan to reflect the progress you've made to date.

It May be Worth Hiring a Separate Business Advisor

Depending on the services offered by your accountant, you may still want to hire a business advisor or coach who will meet with you more regularly. Whereas you may meet with your accountant two or three times a year, you might schedule monthly meetings with a business advisor.

Your advisor's role is to answer your questions, offer advice and guide you through pitfalls. The advisor will also set key performance indicators for you to meet, review your performance against them, and then hold your feet to the fire so that you hit your targets.

The sad truth is that most creative people aren't very good with finances. We're usually not thrilled by spreadsheets and financial formulas. It's not what we think about every day.

That's why you want a business advisor. By going through your numbers, your advisor can point out whether your costs are in line, whether you're billing enough, whether you're profitable on some types of jobs but not on others, whether you're operating as efficiently as you had planned.

The advisor can make recommendations to improve your profitability, optimize your client mix, and perhaps review your staffing. Some advisors are also a good source of leads. They generally have a big network and can be instrumental in introducing you to new clients.

Chapter Takeaways

- Write a short business plan to clarify your thinking about your company's future.
- Get an accountant or business advisor to review your plan for feedback.

- Find the right accountant who understands your business sector and acts as a consultant.
- Your accountant should make you financially literate so that you pay attention to and understand your numbers.
- Consider contracting with a business advisor to keep you on track.
- Periodically compare your performance to your business plan and make adjustments as necessary.

9

YOUR MONEY ATTITUDE

"While money can't buy happiness, it certainly lets you choose your own form of misery."

— Groucho Marx

How Much Money Should You Make?

If you're starting a creative agency, how much money should you make? The short answer, which is somewhat unhelpful, is a lot. You should be going into business to make a lot of money. How much is "a lot"? It all depends, of course. First, let's talk about how people make money and what they give and get in return.

Hobby Money

Many people have hobbies where there is some chance of making money. Maybe you're a painter. You sell some paintings at art shows, to your friends, or contacts on Facebook. Perhaps you have an online gallery. But if you looked at it seriously, your hobby is likely costing you more than you're making.

Obviously, you need other income to live on and to help support your hobby, which brings in a few dollars now and then. But that's okay because really, you just love to paint. You'd do it for nothing, which is a good thing because many months, that's what you're earning.

However, if you're serious about starting a company, you can't treat it like a hobby. Money is not incidental to your company. It's central to its existence. This company will be your primary source of income.

Some people are fortunate enough to turn their hobby into a business. Here are a few hypothetical examples.

There are many filmmakers with films on YouTube. If they have enough followers, they can make money from YouTube and perhaps get some sponsorships. They may earn a few thousand dollars a year.

A few people work hard enough to get millions of followers and make a good living at it. They're often earning hundreds of thousands of dollars, and then there are the superstars making millions. But for most people, it's a hobby that pays little or nothing.

You'll find photographers selling prints on Instagram or Facebook, makers and crafters setting up shop on Etsy, and others selling books and info-products on Amazon. All of these can earn a little money, and very few provide a comfortable living.

Let's say you're a hobby filmmaker on YouTube, and your goal is to transition to becoming a professional filmmaker. In doing that, there must be a definite turning point, a change in perspective, where it goes from casual fun making videos to a serious enterprise working for clients who regularly pay you.

That transition means a lot of things have to change, starting with your perspective on money.

Side Hustle, AKA Freelance Money

Let's assume you have a job, and you're providing freelance content creation as a side hustle. Maybe you're a weekend wedding photographer, a writer who has a few small clients, or a designer doing freelance web work. Perhaps you promote yourself on one of the global outsourcing platforms like Fiverr or Upwork.

You're making some extra money, you're working in the business that could be the foundation of a more significant company, and you may have some portfolio pieces to show prospects.

If you're working solo, it's a pretty simple operation. There's no pressure to earn a lot of money since you're still getting paid from your day job. You can afford to take on smaller clients, charge them what you can, and be happy if you're able to build the business slowly.

Some people working side hustles have definite plans and timelines for throwing the switch—turning that side hustle into the primary income source. Others are happy as employees, making a freelance income to boost their regular pay with no real plans beyond that.

If you've got a side hustle going, it's worth examining your attitude toward it. Turning your side hustle into a full-time company will take a concerted effort.

First will be an in-depth examination of the work you're doing and the money you're getting paid. The temptation is not to take your side hustle that seriously. In most cases, your clients will know it's not your full-time job, so they may look to you for a bargain.

You may get verbal offers to do jobs for $100, and without thinking about it too much, you'll agree. In your mind, it's "extra money," and you figure you could knock the work out in a few hours.

This becomes a very casual way of working. You don't track your hours, and you're probably not charging enough.

If you're planning to make the transition from a side hustle to a full-time gig, you should work your side hustle as if it's already your full-time job.

That means taking more time to define projects, providing detailed written estimates, pricing them correctly, and keeping track of your time to see how much you're making per hour.

Simply put, don't get into the habit of working casually and charging random amounts for projects. That will not serve you well in a full-time company. Start good habits early and build on them for the future when your side hustle becomes full-time.

Employee Money

Let's say you're working for a leading creative agency. Perhaps you're employed as a copywriter or graphic designer. You're good at what you do and are getting paid a decent salary with benefits that reflect your talent and experience.

Your agency has a variety of appealing clients, your colleagues are talented and fun to work with, so you're enjoying your work life. Most days, you work 9–5, sometimes a little more, but you don't mind.

You get an annual review where you usually get a little raise, a bonus, or maybe both. You may even participate in profit sharing. In general, it's a good gig. Your main concern is doing outstanding work for your clients and having excellent portfolio pieces that you can show off should you decide to move to another firm.

If you're in a junior to intermediate position, you'll likely stay there for two or three years before moving on to get a bigger salary increase than just a raise from your annual review.

If you're in a senior position, you'll likely stay longer, assuming everything goes well. You might even get a title, such as Associate Creative Director, which gives you additional responsibility overseeing the work of junior teams.

But as an employee, you mainly worry just about yourself, your day-to-day work, and your career. You're not responsible for the firm's overall profitability, the increasing overhead costs, getting new clients, staff turnover, finding the right suppliers, client reviews, etc.

In other words, even in a senior position making good money, you're an employee, not an owner. You don't have the same responsibilities and concerns as an owner. There's a massive difference, and it's reflected in your take-home pay. As an employee, you likely don't have any chance of making a lot of money, and even if you do, you're still not the owner.

Business Owner Money

Let's get to why you should be aiming to make "a lot" of money as the owner of your business. You are taking on considerable risk. Not so much at the beginning if you're a one-person company, but once you acquire employees and partners, your risk increases.

Remember, statistically, half of small companies are out of business before their fifth anniversary. That's a polite way of saying it. What happens behind the scenes? The owners may have to declare bankruptcy. They may leave trusted suppliers and employees holding the bag. Their credit rating is likely trashed.

They may be subject to lawsuits. So, think of that risk as you consider starting a company.

As your company grows, you might sign up for obligations like office leases. You may buy furniture, equipment, and supplies. (When I think of how much I've paid for dozens of office chairs, desks, and computers over the years.) You hire staff who now count on you. You make promises to clients who also depend on you.

You have to pay for staff benefits beyond salaries if you want to keep the best people. You have to deal with the government for various forms of taxes. You have an accountant, perhaps also a business advisor, and if you need it, a lawyer.

You have to keep the cash flow flowing, week after week, month after month. When it gets hectic, it's you who is working the insane hours plus weekends, eating lunch at your desk, forgoing a long vacation because you can't afford to be away.

When it's not busy, you're losing sleep, wondering how you can get more business because you know your monthly overhead, and it's a daunting number.

There are times when you feel trapped, like you're working for your employees. Wasn't it supposed to be the other way around? After all, if you were just an employee, you could walk away, go work somewhere else, or if you saved up, you could take a year off to travel. That's practically impossible as an owner.

Oh, there are lots of good times too. The congratulatory calls you get when you win new business, happy clients calling you with compliments, talented people who want to work with you and your team. There's industry recognition, awards, maybe even profiles in publications and on websites.

You feel good being able to provide meaningful jobs for your staff. You have fun at the holiday parties that you put on (and gladly pay for).

But don't take too long to celebrate—you're only as good as your last job. Get back to work! And that's why you should be making a lot of money.

But Seriously, How Much is "A Lot of Money"?

Because there are so many different scenarios for company owners, coming up with a specific dollar amount for "a lot of money" is impossible. However, here are a couple of ways to think about it.

How much would you be earning if you were an employee practicing your craft at a top firm? Include any bonuses you would be getting. Take a moment to think about it.

Running a company with employees, you should be making at least two to three times as much to compensate for all of the added risk and responsibility. If that sounds out of reach, it's time to readjust your thinking because that's how much you should be making.

Here's another perspective: if your staff includes senior practitioners (senior designer, senior writer, etc.), you should have a base salary of at least 150 percent of theirs, plus dividends and a significant share of year-end profits. Thinking about it this way is also an excellent test to determine whether you should go from being a solo practitioner to creating a larger company.

If you're a solo practitioner, look at your current income, clients, and business. Ask yourself whether creating a company with more employees or perhaps a partner or two would allow you to earn 150 to 200 percent of what you're making today.

If not, why bother because you're about to take on substantially more responsibility?

The bigger the company, the more the top executives should be earning. It works for Wall Street companies, and it should work for smaller companies, too. When you think about it like this, it also forces you to consider the types of clients and the amount of business you'll need to support this income level.

Chapter Takeaways

- Get comfortable with the money side of business. Build your business so that it compensates you appropriately for the risk you've taken on.
- As an owner, you should be making at least two to three times what a senior practitioner earns.
- The bigger your company, the more you should be taking home. Otherwise, why bother?
- Think about your finances and compensation. You're not running a charity. Make sure your company is profitable and you're well paid.

10

STARTING UP

"Of course you pay the price for your past. That's what credit cards are about."

— Vineet Raj Kapoor

The Most Important Tip When You're Starting Your Own Business

This "precious, but not so secret tip" applies whether you're working as an individual or corporation. And the big tip is: **Keep Your Expenses Down**, especially recurring ones like rents or leases.

Think of recurring expenses as ongoing debts. These are amounts you owe month after month. Before you can pay anything else, you have to pay these. In some cases, these expenses may prevent you from growing your company because you simply can't afford it.

What does this mean in practical terms? Let's review where you can save and where some people blow their budgets.

Office Space. Do You Need It?

For many small companies, the rent and related expenses for office space are the top fixed monthly costs aside from salaries.

If you and your team can work from your homes, you will save thousands of dollars every month. Also, getting an office means signing a lease that you're on the hook for, first and last month's rent upfront, start-up costs such as buying furniture, perhaps paying for renovations to get the office to suit you, and paying for WiFi, an alarm system, and utilities. Setting up an office could cost you tens of thousands of dollars.

If you can work from home, not only are you not paying rent for an office, but you will likely be able to write off part of your home rent or mortgage along with other expenses such as taxes and utilities against the business. Again, speak to your accountant.

In most cases, you calculate the number of square feet of your dedicated office as a percentage of your home and write off that percentage of all eligible expenses.

For many years, I worked out of my home office, which occupied 15 percent of the home's total area. So, I wrote off 15 percent of the mortgage, taxes, utilities, and any other house-related expenses as a business expense against income. It made a big difference.

If you're thinking of a larger company, say more than three people, you might consider renting a small space for a core group and have everyone else working from home. Get a big table so people can come in for meetings or work with you for a while. You want as much flexibility as possible to lower your costs.

What if you and your partner live in a tiny apartment with no room or privacy for an office? You might be better off moving to a bigger home with a room for an office, knowing you can write off part of it, rather than staying in your current apartment and paying for office space.

Do the math to see whether that works for you.

If that's not possible, can you work out of a coffee shop? With a decent pair of headphones, you can cancel out the noise around you, and coffee is nearby. Get there early for the best spot. You can write off the headphones as a business expense.

If you don't like working in coffee shops, how about the local library? They generally have good workstations, decent free WiFi, and they're quiet.

Many towns now have shared working spaces. While they seem cool, they're not cheap. At a minimum, you'll be paying $500 a month for shared space and $1,000 a month or more for a bit more privacy. I would choose this as a last resort if none of the other options work. Your goal is to have as close to zero fixed monthly expenses as possible.

Another option is to look for meeting rooms that you can rent by the hour or day. Everyone can work from home, and you schedule regular meetings to catch up, compare notes, and have lunch together.

Lastly, don't think that you need an office because clients will want to come there. They don't. Clients rarely, if ever, wish to meet anywhere other than their own office.

If they're going to take a break from their office, a nearby coffee shop is usually perfect. Buy them coffee and a muffin. For a big meeting, take them out to a nice lunch.

If you do decide you need office space, shop around. Sometimes you can sublet space that's already furnished and comes with WiFi. See whether other firms have extra space to sublet.

Depending on your location, look for parts of town that aren't trendy or too popular.

Sometimes you can find low-cost space above retail stores. Whatever you decide, try not to burden yourself with significant overhead expenses when you're starting.

New or More Equipment?

I've seen people get very excited when they've finally decided to start their agency. Time for a new beginning, right? Get the latest phone, a new computer, a new scanner, a new printer, a new and better camera, some lights, and so on. Get a shiny new car, put it on a company lease.

Hang on a minute. Really? Are these needs or wants? Did you budget and save for this, or is it all going on your credit card, and you'll be paying interest for years?

Instead, try the minimalist approach. Work with what you have. Or if you need a specific piece of equipment for the job, see whether you can rent it. Bury the cost of the rental in your estimate for the client.

If you're using your car for work, be sure to track the mileage and claim the appropriate expenses. Again, your accountant can guide you here.

Getting into debt right at the beginning puts a lot of pressure on you. There will be times when there's no business coming in the door, yet the bills always appear. Live like a monk—a monk with money in the bank. You'll sleep much better.

Be Conservative in Managing Your Money

One way or another, you have to manage your money to keep yourself out of financial trouble. What do I mean?

Well, some people tend to spend their money as they get it. When times are good, the money seems to flow out as fast as it comes in. When business slows down, uh oh, they're broke. That's no way to run a business. Working with your accountant, you will soon have a grasp of your expenses and what it costs to keep you going month after month.

In the beginning, your most significant expense will likely be you —your salary. How much should your salary be? Of course, that all depends. Did you save before you started your business so that you can live off your savings for the first few months? That way, all the revenue can be used as a cushion.

Ideally, you should have at least three months of operating expenses in cash in the bank (not receivables that you don't yet have) as a cushion at all times. That's not as easy as it sounds and may take some time to build up. Let's say your overhead, including your salary, is $10,000 a month. That means you should set aside $30,000 that you don't touch other than for emergencies. That will be a challenge to save.

Formalize Your Salary and Keep It as Low as Possible

For now, let's assume you're working solo, whether or not you're incorporated. The temptation is to have a casual relationship with the money coming in. That's not the way to do it.

Come up with a number that your business can support. You can change it later. By way of example, let's say you're billing $150,000 a year, or an average of $12,500 a month. Before you look at anything else, you need to set aside money for taxes. To keep the math easy, let's say taxes are 25 percent. That leaves you with $112,500, or $9,375 a month.

Now, assuming you didn't save enough of a cushion in advance, you'll want to build one up for emergencies, so let's say you set aside $1,000 a month. That leaves you with $8,375. Do the math, and you'll see that if you want to build up a cushion of $30,000 at the rate of $1,000 a month, it will take you 30 months or two and a half years to get there.

You've kept your expenses to a minimum by working from home, so they're just $500 a month. Now you're at $7,875 a month. So, what if your salary was $7,000 a month to start? Leave the other $875 a month in the bank.

Then, if everything goes to plan, once or twice a year, in consultation with your accountant, you give yourself a bonus or declare a dividend if you've incorporated.

Why do it this way?

The first reason is discipline. Like all aspects of your business, you want to take a disciplined and conservative approach to the money you take from your company.

Second, your billing and your collection of your invoices may be "lumpy"—in other words, not a smooth flow, but high one month and low the next.

Third, once you've built your cushion, you no longer have to contribute to it, so you may choose to raise your salary a bit, or if possible, leave it in the bank.

As your company grows, assuming it's profitable, you can increase your salary. At that point, you will want the advice of your accountant or a financial planner on the best way to receive this income. You may find that a combination of salary and dividends is the most tax advantageous for you.

Here's a Quick Story to Scare You into Saving

At one point in my second company, we were doing many projects for a corporate client. At the time, this was our biggest client. Everything was fine. They were happy with our work, and we were thrilled to have a steady flow of jobs. They paid in a timely fashion, usually within 30 days, as per our agreement.

Then one day, we noticed they were falling behind in paying invoices. We let it go for a while, assuming we'd get paid any day. Then it was 60 days, and when we weren't looking, it became 90 days.

We were still doing a lot of work for them, and on top of that, we had bills from suppliers for work we had commissioned on their behalf. We were also paying sales taxes on invoices we had billed but not collected.

We called one of our contacts there to talk about it. "We've just switched accounting systems and are working out some glitches." Now, we were at 100 days. They owed us over $250,000, and it was starting to hurt.

At that point, I called the head of the marketing department, with whom we, fortunately, had a good relationship. I explained the issue. He had no idea about the delay in payment and wasn't happy to hear it.

The next day, I got a call from their accounting department to review our invoices to make sure they had all of them in the system. Later that day, we got a check by courier for the full amount. Whew!

Three lessons from that:

1. Things can go wrong, even with the best clients.
2. Have a cushion so you can survive if things do go wrong.
3. Build relationships with clients as high up as possible in case you need help.

The fourth lesson I should have known at the time was that when you start to sense something is going sideways with a client, like they usually pay in 30 days and then they don't, get their attention as soon as possible. Escalate the issue if necessary. Be polite, and don't assume any evil intent, but don't let it go, hoping it will fix itself.

We Need to Talk About Taxes

Taxes are a critical reason you need a disciplined approach to your finances. In most jurisdictions, you are likely looking at two types of corporate taxes: sales taxes that you bill and collect from clients and corporate taxes on your company's profits. Of course, the third tax is your personal income tax, but let's focus on the corporate taxes for now.

Depending on where you do business and pay your taxes and the size of your business, these taxes might be due monthly, quarterly, or annually. Whatever the case, you cannot spend that money. You need to put it aside to pay your taxes in a timely fashion.

Do not allow yourself to fall behind and get on the wrong side of the government. Do not try to avoid or evade taxes. Governments are merciless. They will get their money, and if you fall too far behind, they'll grab it out of your bank account without warning, and in some cases, with a penalty.

You may also be subject to an audit, a huge distraction, and a waste of time and money. And, by the way, if you get on their wrong side, they can audit you as often as they like.

So, stay up to date with your taxes. Be extraordinarily disciplined and pay on time.

Chapter Takeaways

- Rule #1: Keep your expenses down. Pay yourself as little as reasonable to start. You can adjust later.
- Think hard about your working arrangements. If you and your team can work from home, you'll have substantial savings every month.
- Stay out of debt. You'll have enough to think about without that looming over your head. Buy equipment only when necessary and when you can pay for it.
- Build a cushion of three months' expenses in the bank. Work hard to maintain it.
- If you sense a problem with a client paying you, get in touch immediately. Don't let it slide.
- Pay your taxes on time without fail.

11

RUNNING YOUR AGENCY

"Be steady and well-ordered in your life so that you can be fierce and original in your work."

— Gustave Flaubert

Think in Systems

Some people are naturally organized; others are not. Organized people usually have tidy desks and well-structured folders and files on their computers. Others...well, it's a little more all over the place with bits of paper and scribbled notes. Many people in creative agencies fall into the second category.

That's okay, but if you're not organized by nature, and you want to run a company, even a one-person company, you're going to need some help. Even if you are organized, there are a few systems you need to have in place:

I. A bookkeeping/accounting system.

2. A system for tracking jobs, including time tracking, expenses, estimates, and invoices.
3. A communications platform if your company grows beyond a few people.
4. A calendar/task list program to help track your deadlines, calls, and tasks. Use the notifications to remind you in advance. This may be included in your communications platform. I've been using Google Calendar but have also used Apple Calendar. Both are free and work well. There are also many other choices. Pick one and use it consistently.

Being Organized Now Avoids Problems Later

You may be tempted to put off getting organized, thinking that you'll do it when you need it. I don't recommend that approach. Ideally, you want to look into the future and realize the problems you'll run into if you're disorganized.

For example, if you don't have a consistent method for estimating and invoicing, you could be losing work (whoops, forgot to send them an estimate) or doing the job but not getting paid because you didn't send an invoice. Get your systems in place early and use them consistently.

You want to create Standard Operating Procedures. These are consistent, proven methods to do all of the many tasks it takes to run your company. The more organized you are, the more you can focus on your creative work.

Figure Out How You're Going to Handle Accounting

Your day-to-day accounting needs are going to depend on the size of your company. Whatever your situation is, start by speaking to your accountant. What will the accountant want in order to complete your year-end books and file your taxes? Would your accountant prefer that you use a specific accounting package to integrate with theirs?

If you do a bit of research, you'll find two or three top accounting systems for small companies. Your accountant will likely be familiar with them. Whatever he or she recommends, do that. Even if you're a solo operator, you may as well start on a system that can grow with you. In the past, we've used Quickbooks and MYOB, but there are many others.

When Do You Hire a Bookkeeper?

Let's assume that based on your accountant's recommendation, you've decided on accounting software. Generally, it's pretty easy to use, and you might be tempted to start using it yourself.

I would find someone (a recommendation from your accountant, perhaps) to come in as often as necessary to do your bookkeeping. Work out whatever makes sense at the time.

When my partners and I started our company, we did our own estimates, proposals, and invoices and left them in a tray for filing by our bookkeeper, along with any relevant mail, such as bills and bank statements.

The bookkeeper came in for one day every two weeks to enter everything into our accounting software, pay bills, and produce reports for us to review. As we got busier, we changed the schedule to once a week. Then, after a few years, we hired a full-time bookkeeper who also did the invoicing.

The other benefit of having a bookkeeper is that they will sit down with you and review the reports they give you. Sometimes, you focus so much on your day-to-day work, you forget to look at the finances—money in the bank, money coming in, receivables you need to chase, bills you should pay.

You can adjust your bookkeeping requirements as you grow. But once you get beyond a one-person company, I wouldn't try to do it myself. Your time is better used working on projects and getting new business.

Security and Your Bookkeeper

Allow me to fabricate a statistic: I'll guess that 99 percent of book-keepers are completely honest. However, that means that some aren't and could steal your money and generally wreak havoc on your company. A favorite fraud technique is for a bookkeeper to set up a company, create invoices from that company to your company, and issue payments.

It makes sense that you or one of your partners are the only ones who can authorize payments and sign checks.

Make sure you know who is getting paid, what it's for, and that the amount matches the invoice. For electronic payments, you should get a copy of the printout that highlights which payments were made to whom, for what.

When you have your regular meetings with your bookkeeper, have him or her take you through everything that's coming in or going out. You should also take the time to review your bank statements to make sure they align with outgoing payments.

Track Time and Expenses

From the beginning, you'll want software that records job details, records the time of people working on each job, keeps track of expenses, and gives you reports on billing, profitability, etc.

I've used FunctionFox in my previous companies, and I know others are using Harvest or Trello—there are many choices. Sign up for demo accounts and read reviews to see which one suits you.

Read the section on time sheets to fully understand why you want to track time, even when you're working solo.

You May Need More Collaborative Software Than Email

If there are just a few of you, email will likely be sufficient for sending detailed information to each other. But once you work in larger groups, think about more sophisticated communication platforms that allow better collaboration and give you threaded discussions, calendar functions, task lists, project reports, and so on.

In the past, I've used Slack and Asana, which are both quite popular.

A tip on communicating in the office: try to settle on one way to communicate with each other about client work. Try not to use Slack, email, text, and other platforms at the same time. You'll always be searching for that critical information. It's a huge waste of time. If you're on Slack, Asana, or another platform, stick to that.

Be Creative in Your Work, but Predictable in Your Processes

You look at life with a creative focus. Your job is to come up with innovative solutions to your clients' communications and marketing challenges.

However, you should deliver your creative ideas within a consistent, predictable framework. You need to develop and refine processes for how you do the things you do most often. Otherwise, you'll waste time and create frustration for yourself and everyone around you. And that means chaos.

To put it another way, you may wear the most creative wardrobe, but when you get dressed every morning, you want to know you'll find your socks and underwear in the same drawer.

Processes for creative agencies include:

- How you structure and write your estimates and invoices.
- How you open a job.
- How you brief anyone who will work on it.
- How you present to the client.
- How you follow through with revisions and production.
- Once you finish a job, how you close it out and manage any related files.

For example, let's look at the process of opening a job once you have an approved estimate. What happens first, and who does it? The steps might include:

- Brief a project manager on the details of the job.
- The project manager enters the pertinent details into the job-tracking software.
- The project manager creates a new folder on your central file server to store all relevant briefing documents and other related files.
- The project manager creates a work-back schedule with critical dates (internal presentation, client presentations, final deliverables) in the group calendar.
- Together with the project manager, you schedule a briefing meeting for the creative team assigned to this project.
- The project manager (or bookkeeper) writes and sends the deposit invoice (if appropriate).

And then the job gets underway. Whatever process you come up with should become engrained so that it's second nature. If you look at these hypothetical steps, you'll see some of the underlying structure. This process assumes:

- There is job-tracking software. Everyone knows that they'll find project details here. The file for each project is organized in a consistent manner.
- There is a central file server. This is where files for projects are kept. It may be a server you maintain in your workspace or an online service such as Dropbox.
- There is a group calendar to keep track of critical dates. This could be part of the job-tracking software, communications platform, or another online calendaring system.
- There is a process for creating invoices when agreed-upon milestones are met. For example, this may include invoicing for deposits and progress billing.

Processes Are for You but Mainly for Your Employees

No matter how you run your personal life, your business life must be organized and process-driven.

Your employees are looking to you for leadership and guidance, and a big part of that is based on consistent processes. Employees want to know, "This is how we do things."

Try to keep your processes streamlined and straightforward. You want everyone in your agency to learn these processes and start working with them quickly.

Most of all, your employees want certainty. To them, certainty feels like the company's leaders know what they're doing.

Being organized frees up everyone to be creative. You and your employees can focus on the tasks at hand. You won't waste time looking for files, or worse yet, working on the wrong version of a file. They will appreciate consistent, process-driven structure and discipline.

Having processes in place allows you to scale. If you're constantly figuring out how you do the most basic tasks, you'll be forever spinning your wheels.

Processes Let You Take Vacations

With defined processes that employees understand and follow, you can feel more confident that staff will do their jobs in a consistent manner. That means you don't personally have to be involved in every project.

Your company should operate like a sophisticated assembly line. There are variations for different types of jobs, but basically, all the steps are defined, with one step following another.

And that means you can take your holidays without worrying about everything falling apart.

Rules for Internal Meetings

Once your company starts growing, you're sure to have internal meetings, whether face-to-face or online. Keep in mind that poorly run meetings can suck up a lot of time, making them very expensive. Take the billing rate for everyone in the meeting, then multiply that by the amount of time the meeting takes. It's probably a high number.

You should only hold a meeting if you want dialogue from the others.

If you're simply conveying information that doesn't need feedback, an email or note on your communications platform is likely more effective.

Here are some meeting rules to follow:

- Only invite people whose input or updates you need. If you're planning a project, only ask those who have a stake in it. If the meeting's purpose is to make a decision, only invite those whose opinions will be considered.
- For short meetings such as project updates with only a few people, make them stand-up meetings. Everyone stands, no one sits. It keeps people focused on the topic, and the meeting will go more quickly.
- Longer meetings need an agenda circulated well in advance of the meeting, preferably 24 hours ahead. By writing the agenda, you'll clarify your thinking about the meeting and the desired outcomes. By providing it a day in advance, recipients can review it and have time to do any necessary preparations before the meeting.
- From your agenda, attendees should understand the purpose of the meeting and prepare for it if necessary. Are they expected to bring anything to the discussion? If so, outline this in your agenda. You may want to have a quick conversation with them ahead of the meeting to help them prepare.
- Be strict on start and end times. Start your meetings precisely on time—not five, ten, or fifteen minutes late. Employees will take their cue from you. If they're late once, they should be too embarrassed to be late again. If someone is perpetually late, you need to talk to them. And you, as the boss, must be punctual. Don't pull a power trip and have everyone waiting for you. It's disrespectful and shows a lack of leadership.

- Be focused. This is not the time to talk about weekend plans or last night's game. Stick to the agenda.
- Determine the duration of the meeting ahead of time and let attendees know. It will focus the group. Meetings don't have to be an hour. Often, thirty or forty minutes will do. Pick a duration and stick to it. Have a timer running, visible to everyone.
- Meetings need follow-ups. Someone in the group, likely a project manager, should take detailed notes and ensure everyone knows what the next steps are, complete with deadlines. This should be reviewed during the last ten minutes of the meeting and distributed afterward. Everyone should know "who will do what by when?"
- If it's a face-to-face meeting, no phones or laptops in the meeting, except the notetaker's laptop. No phone calls, texts, or checking emails. It's distracting. If someone needs to check email frequently, maybe they shouldn't be in the meeting.

Tips to Encourage Meeting Efficiency

Here are two easy ways to promote meeting efficiency: hold them just before lunch or toward the end of the day, which puts a natural limit on how long the meeting runs.

Don't provide refreshments for internal face-to-face meetings. When someone has to choose just the right donut and then run out to get a coffee, it slows everything down.

Chapter Takeaways

- Think in systems and then use the right software platforms to help you create and maintain processes to run your company.

- Define your processes, try them out, fine-tune them and then abide by them. Your employees will appreciate the guidance, and you'll have fewer on-the-fly decisions to make.
- Get a bookkeeper to take care of the financial record keeping.
- Decide how often the bookkeeper comes in. Adjust as necessary.
- Run your internal meetings efficiently. They're expensive.

12

DECISION-MAKING

"Truly successful decision-making relies on a balance between deliberate and instinctive thinking."

— Malcolm Gladwell

Leaders Make Decisions

Real leaders make decisions. That may sound self-evident, but if you've ever worked for someone who procrastinates endlessly or changes his mind frequently, you'll appreciate someone who decides and then moves forward.

Some decisions are easy, others are hard. All decisions have consequences. You'll often wish you had additional information to help you decide, but the reality is that many times, you won't have the perfect amount of data. You simply have to decide based on the information you have.

Your indecision means others are waiting and frozen in place until you've made up your mind. You'll find making a decision brings relief. Once you've done it, the logjam has been broken, and now everyone can move forward.

How can you improve your decision-making? Give yourself a deadline and communicate it to others. Now you'll be held to it. For a relatively small decision, make your deadline by the end of the day. Before the day is over, you will decide and let all relevant people know of your conclusion.

For a more significant decision, one that requires research and input from others, give yourself one or two weeks. Let others who are affected by your decision know of your timetable. Assign some of the research to team members, schedule a meeting to review and discuss your thinking before making a decision, and then before the deadline, pull the trigger.

Apply the Jeff Bezos Theory to Decision-Making

Recently, I read an article describing one of Jeff Bezos's philosophies on decision-making at Amazon. Bezos divided decisions into two categories to encourage his executives to make decisions as quickly as possible. He called the categories "one-way doors" and "two-way doors."[1]

A one-way door only swings one way. It's the kind of decision that once you make it, you can't easily go back. There's no unmaking it without great cost or turmoil.

In our world, a one-way door decision might be taking on a partner in your business. Once you've done that, it's difficult to undo without a lot of expense, legal issues, and potentially breaking up your company.

So, a one-way door decision deserves more time and input. But at some point, in the relatively near future, that decision gets made. Just calling something a one-way door decision doesn't give anyone at Amazon the right not to make that decision. The same should apply to you.

If you think about it, though, most decisions are two-way doors. You can undo them. You can change your mind. Yes, there may be some costs involved, usually in time and money, but it's not catastrophic or life-changing.

For example, let's say you want to start using an online time sheet management system. With a little bit of research, you'll find at least a half dozen that might do the job.

You'll see reviews, demos, tutorials, testimonials, etc., to help you decide. You might call colleagues to ask what they're using. You'll likely be able to sign up for free demo accounts. You could sign up for two or three demo accounts simultaneously and run them all through a few exercises.

Give yourself a deadline of a few days, and then choose one. Sure, you could take a month or more to decide, but why?

Most of these platforms will let you pay by the month, so pick one and use it for a few months. Get accustomed to the functions.

What's the worst that can happen? You change your mind. You don't like the one you chose. But at least you will now have a better idea of what you're looking for. You'll likely be able to export your data and import it into another system. A little trouble, but not a major deal.

The best-case scenario is that the first system you chose works fine for your company, you've become much more efficient, your employees know how to use it, and it's one less thing on your dreaded To-Do List. You've decided, and now you and your employees can move forward.

The worst-case scenario is that you have to try another system, and you already have a runner-up because you tested a few simultaneously. Now it's time to try your second favorite.

Chapter Takeaways

- Leaders make decisions, often with imperfect information. Procrastination leaves everything up in the air. A decision lets you and those involved move forward.
- As the boss, you are the one who must make the critical decisions. Get used to it.

---

1. Jeff Haden, "Amazon Founder Jeff Bezos: This Is How Successful People Make Such Smart Decisions," *Inc.*, December 3, 2018. https://www.inc.com/jeff-haden/amazon-founder-jeff-bezos-this-is-how-successful-people-make-such-smart-decisions.html.

13

DEFINING YOUR SERVICES

```
"We are our choices."
```

— Jean-Paul Sartre

Think Hard About Your Service Offerings

Let's say you're currently a graphic designer employed full time by a creative agency. You create layouts for various projects, including websites, email campaigns, and social media.

But if you think about it, you'll realize that what you're doing is just one part of a more significant project. The agency you work for doesn't just sell website designs, email campaign designs, and social media graphics. They sell complete projects.

So, in the case of a website, the agency worked with the client on the overall site strategy, the site architecture, the messages, the technology, the design, right up to and including launching the site.

Most of the time, that's what the client wants and is actually buying—the complete deliverable from beginning to end. When you start your company, your clients are going to want the same thing: complete deliverables. You need to have a plan to define and then create those projects.

As an example, think about Facebook advertising campaigns. To run one of these campaigns, clients need a strategy, messages, designs, perhaps some animation or video, integration with website landing pages, someone to set up the campaign on Facebook, including target markets, budgets, frequency, reporting... and rinse and repeat over and over again.

This is one of the most significant leaps you have to make—from being an employee where you provided part of the solution, to starting your own company where your clients expect the complete project. Be very clear on what your services will consist of and who the clients are for those offerings.

In some cases, clients may want to do parts of the project with their in-house staff or other suppliers. But I think you need to be prepared to deliver the complete service. Taking on the full project means you have more control. It also translates into higher billings.

Depending on the elements you need for a service, you may want to work with freelancers, contractors, or other specialty companies.

My companies took care of all communications requirements up to and including front-end programming of websites in-house and worked with contractors for more complex systems integration requirements.

But Couldn't You Just Be a Freelance Writer, Designer, Social Media Marketer?

Yes, of course, you could. There are many solo practitioners offering just those services. I worked freelance as a copywriter for six years and built up a substantial list of corporate clients.

But even early on, clients would ask whether I had a graphic designer to help with the project. Then they wanted to know if I had web programmers to bring to the project. The client needed the whole project done, and writing was just part of it. That's why I decided to form a bigger agency.

This is where 1+1 truly equals 3. By teaming up with just one person to complement your skill set, you are seen as much more than two individuals. You are now a team able to take on more than before.

Working solo, you're missing out on opportunities for more significant projects. Once projects get to a certain size and degree of complexity, clients are looking for companies that can deliver everything they need.

Think of it from their perspective. It's easier for them to brief one company for the whole job, and get one estimate for everything than to brief several individuals, receive and approve separate estimates and keep track of the coordination, budgets, and billing.

Also, think about this. If you're working solo, you will only get called for the type of work you perform. In other words, if you're a writer, you'll get called for writing projects. Makes sense.

But suppose you had a bigger company and were known for offering complete projects (writing and design, or writing and design and production). In that case, you could benefit from projects where there wasn't any writing, but your company gets the project anyway because you provide all the other services.

In theory, you could, in fact, do the writing or design for a big project. But in reality, you'll often get passed over because the client is looking for an all-in-one provider.

There were many projects in my companies where we didn't do the writing (for example, highly technical medical writing by doctors and researchers). Still, we produced the brochures, books, presentations, and websites that the client needed. As a writer and company owner, I benefited from those projects.

Also, consider that it's much easier for clients to compare your rates or estimates to competitors if you only offer one service. They can quickly get multiple estimates on a simple writing job. The ease of getting those multiple estimates means that it becomes a more competitive market for you.

However, it's a lot more work for them to obtain competitive estimates on complex projects where there are many pieces to the puzzle. As much as possible, you want to get out of the competitive marketplace. You want to encourage clients to give you the whole project, which also makes their lives easier.

Define Deliverables at an Expert Level

As you grow, you'll want to carefully consider how you define your deliverables to ensure you can provide whatever you're selling at an expert level.

Let's look at some of the many aspects of e-commerce websites as an example. If you're building these types of sites, how do you define your expertise? Do you offer just the programming, or can you provide the design and writing? Are you an expert on one type of platform, say WordPress, or can you offer expertise on various platforms such as Shopify, Wix, or SiteCore?

Do you feel comfortable offering expertise in SEO? What about supporting ongoing marketing campaigns?

It's doubtful that one person will be capable of delivering expert consulting for all aspects of this type of project. Think about where your expertise begins and ends and where you'll have to partner with another company, bring in a consultant, or expand your company's size if you want to deliver the entire project.

However you choose to do this, it is not the time to fake it. Claiming expertise that you don't have is a sure way to lose clients.

Bundle Your Services: Make it Easy for Clients and More Profitable for You

After you've done a few projects of the same type, you'll know all of the elements you need to deliver a complete assignment.

For example, for an email campaign, you need writing, design, formatting of the emails, list segmentation and management, email deployment, monitoring, reporting, and creation of one or more landing pages.

You may also want to create a funnel of follow-up emails that need to be deployed and monitored. Finally, you'll need analysis and a summary report of the campaign.

Consider bundling all the tasks related to a project like this and offering the bundle for a set price. Some people refer to it as "pro-ductizing," turning a set of services or products into a single product (like a three-course dinner special). Remember to include rounds of revisions, and whatever else will be involved in the project before coming up with a bottom-line number.

Bundling makes it easier for clients to manage their budgets, and it gives you control over the elements of the offer.

Bundled services are especially useful for small business clients. They don't have to think about all the parts of a campaign they need since you've done it for them.

So, in the case of the emails, there could be a base price of $X for each campaign, plus $X per deployment.

If you're creating images for social media, think about whether you could offer to manage their campaigns and provide the images, writing, monitoring, responses, and regular updates. That might mean a cost per photograph, design, copywriting, and a monthly fee for managing campaigns.

In general, try to think of campaigns rather than single projects. Often clients only consider their immediate requirements, not what they'll need for the next few months.

Also, if you're planning for multiple versions, you should think of creating a template first, which can be more easily used throughout the campaign.

Whichever way you decide to tackle this, think about the services you offer. Consider how you could bundle them to make it easier for clients to sign off while giving you the assurance that you're managing everything for them to be a success.

Typical bundles include:

- Multi-layered email campaign with landing pages
- Print ad plus direct mail
- Trade show displays and handouts
- Social media campaign leading to email sign up on landing page
- Social media assets such as video and photography used over many platforms, all pointing to a landing page, with email sign up

You Can Define Your Services by Media or Technology

Although many creative agencies tend to be generalists, you can decide to narrow your service offerings by media or technology.

For example, there are now many small agencies that focus just on social media. They don't build websites or run email campaigns. They just create and manage social media programs. Others focus only on email campaigns. Again, they exclude everything else and become known for their expertise in email marketing.

But even within that type of narrow focus, there are numerous deliverables that will require different levels of expertise and that you could bundle into productized services.

For example, in an agency focused on social media, some team members would be tasked with the creative. However, there are also essential elements of strategy and analytics required.

Ideally, the agency would deliver the complete package. It will likely take a small group to offer these types of packages unless you happen to have a graphic designer who's also an expert in all of the requirements (not very likely).

If you define yourself by media or technology, be prepared that if you're approaching larger corporate clients, you may be competing against big agency groups who provide these services along with a complete offering of communications services.

So, you may find your three-person email marketing agency up against global giants who want to keep the email marketing assignments as part of their deliverables to the client.

On the other hand, as a specialist provider, you may be called by larger creative agencies to work as a supplier to them. For example, they may not have very sophisticated in-house social media capabilities, so they'll call your social media agency to work as part of their team.

There are upsides and drawbacks to this. First, the upsides: it's income, and you'll likely be working for larger clients. So, you may see it as an opportunity to add to your revenue, raise your profile and work together with a prominent partner for a high-profile client.

But potentially, there are significant drawbacks, too. They may want your services at a lower price than you're comfortable with because they will mark it up before billing to the client.

So, they want the "wholesale" price rather than the "retail" price you usually charge your clients. Then, remember that the client is not your client but rather the agency's client. You may or may not ever have direct communication with the client. That means you're always getting the agency's interpretation of what the client wants or needs, which may skew the message.

It can also be a very inefficient working arrangement. There will likely be an extra step in every communication—from you to the agency to the client. Then it's from the client back to the agency back to you. It's not ideal.

And lastly, the agency may not want the world to know that they didn't provide this service in-house, so as part of your agreement with them, they'll prohibit you from showing this on your website as client work. Watch out for clauses of that nature in any contract you may sign.

As usual, it's always best to have your own direct clients. More money, more control, and much more efficiency.

The Communications World Keeps Evolving—You Need to Keep Up

Every year it seems there's a new platform—hello TikTok, hello Clubhouse—being used for commercial purposes. Depending on who your clients are, you may want to explore using these platforms to reach specific segments of your clients' audiences.

Aside from new platforms, there are also broad communications trends. For years, there has been a move from print to electronic communications.

Simultaneously, video has become much more important, whether on standalone video platforms such as YouTube or Vimeo, or embedded into Facebook, Instagram, or websites.

This doesn't mean you have to be all things to all clients and reach for every shiny new toy. But you should make it your job to stay current with technology or techniques that may be of interest to your clients.

Suppose you decide to integrate new technologies into your offerings. In that case, you should do substantial research to familiarize yourself with the requirements and perhaps contract with a specialist for at least your first few projects.

You can decide whether you'll learn enough working together to bring the skill set in-house, whether it's something you'll continue to contract for, or whether you want to continue with it at all. You may try it and decide it's outside of your offerings.

Resist the temptation to wander into a new technology without being completely confident that you can deliver at a professional level. Don't experiment on client projects. Clients will pay you for what you've already done before. They'll want to see proof that you can actually deliver.

If you're intrigued by a new platform, try it for yourself first. Set up a private test to understand what's required. Perhaps you can integrate it into your promotional channels. Messing up on a project where you're learning on your client's dime puts your entire relationship in jeopardy.

In my agencies, I made sure we were aware of new communications platforms and tools as they emerged to decide whether to make them part of our offering.

Chapter Takeaways

- Define your service offerings. Know what you do or don't provide. Be sure you know how you're going to deliver them—whether with staff, contractors, or freelancers. This can evolve over time.
- Wherever possible, bundle your services. Think of it as "productizing" so that you can sell the same set of services over and over again.
- You may decide to define your services by media or technology. Figure out how you're going to approach clients. Direct clients are better than working as a supplier to agencies.
- If you're getting into new technologies, be confident that you can deliver professionally. Try them for yourself first. Don't experiment on client projects.

14

WORKING WITH CLIENTS

"Great artists need great clients."

— I. M. Pei

Clients vs. Projects—Learn the Difference

When you're starting your agency and looking for work, you'll do many one-off projects. These are jobs where someone needs a logo, a few photographs, or a website. Once that's done, you're finished. There's little chance of ongoing work because they don't have any further requirements.

And that's okay. Sometimes single projects give you a chance to do great work and have a sample for your portfolio. Aside from that, it's revenue.

However, a steady diet of one-off projects is a hard way to grow a business. For every project, you'll have to learn about the company, how they work, their preferences, approval processes, budget, and so on. And just when you've gotten to know each other, it's over.

In general, what you should be looking for are clients. These are companies and organizations that have an ongoing need for the type of work you do. If your company creates videos, you want clients where videos are central to their marketing efforts, and they need many videos throughout the year.

It seems obvious, but I've seen too many people in the business continually chasing single projects that never turn into clients simply because they're one-off assignments. They're making videos for pizza parlors, coffee shops, or hair salons, but their agency never grows into anything.

Similarly, I see many consultants telling creative agencies how they should pitch projects and the magic words to say during the pitch to get the maximum rate for the job. They tell agency owners you have to hustle, hustle, hustle to the point where you begin to think that's the job.

I think there's a better way. For me, the key to success in this business is to get the right clients who give you many projects year after year.

Your job is to keep those clients happy. Focus on building and nurturing relationships. That way, you'll spend more time on billable work, less time on pitches. Life is so much easier that way.

In my companies, our key clients gave us project after project. Many times, we'd be working on five to ten projects for the same client. We didn't have to pitch for each project. They just came to us. They looked on us as their "agency of record" even though we had no overriding agency agreement.

It was all based on good relationships and consistently turning out great work.

Every Client Starts with a Project

Even after you find a company or organization that may have a lot of work for you, you should know that as a smaller company, your way into that client is to do a project. It's not like the big ad agencies where the client awards you the whole account. In your case, they'll try you out by giving you a project with no further commitment.

Assuming everyone loves your work and is happy with the pricing, they'll give you another project and then another one. At this stage, you begin to understand each other better, and the working relationship gets more comfortable. They start counting on you to deliver their campaigns.

But make no mistake, if you don't impress them on that first project, you won't likely get a second one. Even if you get to the point where you're doing regular business together, you can't let up. You are still only as good as your last project.

There are no guarantees or contracts that say the client is obligated to work with you.

Even if there was a contract, it's easily broken. These types of arrangements are always "at the company's pleasure." In other words, they can break it whenever and for whatever reason they like.

You always have to be on your toes to feed and maintain that client relationship. There's plenty of competition knocking on the client's door looking to get the same work you're doing.

So, keep in mind that although every client starts with a project, not all projects turn into clients. As you're pursuing new business, make sure you're going after the right companies.

If there's one key lesson for you to take away from this book, it's this: you should be looking for clients that can give you many projects without you having to pitch and compete for each one.

It's tough to grow a company based on constant hustling and doing just one or two projects for every successful pitch.

Businesses Where There Are Only Projects, No Clients

There are some types of businesses where there are only projects, no ongoing clients. It's not my kind of business (can you tell?), but I know some who are successful at it. The obvious requirement here is strong marketing and sales because you're always searching for new jobs.

If you're in this type of market, consider how you can expand the products and services that your customers can buy from you.

For example, a wedding photographer could emphasize that they also photograph special occasions like holidays, anniversaries, graduations, babies, family birthdays, pets, and more. This still keeps it in the realm of photographing people who are celebrating. That might change how you brand and position yourself.

Maybe instead of a wedding photographer, you become a "life celebrations" photographer. You're not taking pictures of a singular event, you're making memories for the whole family through the years.

If you're a web developer, can you turn the initial site build into a retainer for ongoing updates and maintenance? Can you provide content?

If your business consists of many one-time projects, you have to find ways to maximize each opportunity and get at least a few projects from each customer. And you need to be exceptionally good at marketing and generating word of mouth to keep the leads coming in.

Large Corporate Clients vs. Small Business Clients

It may sound like I'm not keen on small business clients. With my background, I am admittedly most comfortable with larger corporate clients. However, I have had and continue to work with small business clients.

If you're going to work with small business clients, I think you should have the same criteria as you would for larger clients.

This means:

1. They have budgets set aside for the types of projects you do, and over time they will have many projects. The budgets may be smaller, but they're appropriate for the projects.
2. The work that you do for them is vital to their company. You want clients who understand that marketing and communications drive their businesses. If they don't honestly believe that it matters to them, they will always resist.
3. They're comfortable talking about money. This can be a critical differentiator between small and large businesses. In a small business, the money is often the owner's money, and they may be very protective of it, to the point of not wanting to discuss budgets.
4. In a large corporation, the money comes from the company, not the person you're dealing with. Large companies have marketing budgets that they need to spend.
5. They communicate clearly and give you briefs that make sense, preferably in writing. They provide you with

materials that they have, and you need. They understand or are willing to learn how project scope relates to timelines and budgets.

Large Clients Have More Money—It's as Simple as That

Here's a point that is so obvious, it's often overlooked. Big companies have much more money for marketing than small companies. A large company could have a marketing budget of many millions of dollars. In a small company, it's likely tens of thousands of dollars.

Having just a piece of a large company's marketing budget is generally more than having the entire small company budget.

So, imagine that two companies wanted to do a big production video. Let's say you estimated it at $50,000. For a large corporation, that's a tiny fraction of their annual budget.

For a small company, it could be their entire budget. It's easier for the large company's marketing manager to agree to that project than the small company owner.

Now, it might be harder for you to become a supplier to a large company than a smaller one. But it's entirely possible, and when you do, the payoff will be much greater. In my experience, it's worth the effort.

Another Key Difference Between Large and Small Business Clients

Typically, people working in marketing and communications roles in larger companies get paid more than those working in smaller companies. They likely have university degrees, and if they have a job with an impressive title, they have years of experience.

Think of it this way: someone making $150,000 to $200,000 a year is not working on nickel-and-dime projects.

Why would you care about that?

From my observation, they have a different outlook on money and what things cost. They are more professional and more experienced than someone working in an admin function in a smaller company.

They're spending company budgets dedicated to the deliverables they're responsible for. They don't tend to quibble over every dollar. It's more important that they can count on you to deliver successful projects than to save $500 on a $50,000 job.

While the project is in progress, they generally appreciate the steps you have to go through to get to the result, and they're comfortable knowing that processes cost money. They don't expect you to jump right to the conclusion.

For them, the processes also act as insurance. They know you've done your homework and that you've worked through iterations to get to the proposed solution. They understand the process and can explain it to others if need be.

That doesn't mean that they throw money around recklessly. You may still have to explain the rationale behind your estimates, and you may get some pushback. But in general, it's not personal, it's just business.

Of course, there are exceptions to every instance, but this is how it's played out for me.

Help Your Small Business Clients Look at the Big Picture

You make it easier for small business clients if you encourage them to see beyond immediate requirements. Think about launching one extensive campaign over a period of time rather than a series of smaller, single projects.

For example, instead of the job of creating a design and message for a Facebook post, you'll want to encourage them to look at a Facebook campaign that runs over a few months to show them how it rolls out and what phases you might go through over the campaign's duration.

For you and the client, this becomes one project with phases rather than a series of individual projects. One project with five stages is much easier and more cost-effective than five small projects in a row.

Keep in mind that for most small business clients, marketing is only one hat they wear while running their business. The more professional guidance you can bring to it, the easier their job, which makes your work more efficient too.

An Example of an Ideal Small Business Client

For many years, we worked with a client who was the agent and distributor for a European brand of paper used by printers of magazines, brochures, and books. That type of white paper is virtually a commodity, and the competition from paper manufacturers around the world was fierce.

This client understood how marketing, positioning, and imagery could highlight his papers' unique qualities and differentiate him from his competitors.

Although he had a small operation of three people in the office and a few salespeople on the road, he was a consummate marketing professional. We discussed budgets, timelines, goals, opportunities, his competition, in fact, everything about his business.

We looked for ways to maximize his budget and make him look much more prominent in the marketplace than he actually was. Our creative approaches were fresh, and in short order, all of his potential customers knew who he was and the product lines he represented.

For us, this was the ideal small business client. He was enthusiastic, open with information, and understood the necessity of marketing for his company. He didn't have unlimited budgets, but they were appropriate for the campaigns we ran.

Our relationship ended when his European parent company bought him out of his contract. Perhaps they thought with his success, he was doing too well, making too much money, and they could take over.

What did he hand over when they bought his company? An envelope with his marketing materials saved onto a few CDs.

The "Opportunity Document"—A Way to Start Working with Small Clients

One of the challenges of working with small clients is that the person you're working with is often the owner who is in charge of everything. So, marketing, communications, and advertising are just a few of many things the owner does.

In all likelihood, owners haven't taken the time to look at their business from the 50,000-foot level. They're so busy, so close to the everyday requirements, that they don't have a minute to look up and see the possibilities.

An Opportunity Document is an excellent way to start working with such a client. It also gives you much of the information you'll need as you work together.

An Opportunity Document is a summary of the opportunity as you see it for the client to maximize the company's presence and grow in its sector over the next few years.

This is a project you should charge for. It might be the one time where you consciously reduce your fees a little, say by 20 percent. Why would you do this? Because the Opportunity Document will likely be a learning exercise for you too and uncover many future projects.

To do this type of project, you or someone on your team must be very good at research, compiling information, distilling it, and coming to conclusions.

This can be quite time-consuming. Don't underestimate it. Here are examples of what we would include in our Opportunity Documents:

- Introduction to give the reader an understanding of what this document addresses.
- Objectives—what we hope to accomplish in the document.
- Target audiences, which includes a breakdown of all the target audiences we want to appeal to—in addition to external audiences, it would consist of internal audiences like their employees, sales force, or reps.
- Profile of each audience, including their issues or concerns, messages to each audience, benefits to the audience, support for the benefits, questions about the audience.
- The marketing and media vehicles under consideration.
- A breakdown of how we would use each medium to address each specific audience.
- A rough budget allocation for each medium in order of priority.
- Competitive brand overview where we identified the top

competitors in the market, gathered their materials from all media, and commented on their look and feel, messaging, activities (promotions, etc.). In this, we included the client's materials so they could see side-by-side comparisons of how they stacked up.

- Then we looked at "comparative brands." These are brands in other businesses that appeal to our customers. Knowing our customers, we would choose, for example, a car company, clothing brand, specialty food, mobile phone, etc., to evaluate how they speak to these same customers. It's a fascinating exercise for a business owner to step outside of his industry and look at other types of companies appealing to his customers.

Think about proposing an Opportunity Document in the early stages of working with a new client. It opens up a much broader discussion with the client and helps prioritize marketing campaigns going forward.

Over Time, Narrow Your Focus for Client Types

When you start your agency, you'll find yourself working for all kinds of clients. You're still feeling your way around, and besides, you likely need the work and the money. At that stage, you're grateful for every project, and you're not yet in a good position to turn down work.

But soon, you should be narrowing down the types of clients you work for. If this doesn't happen naturally, I think you should actively encourage it.

You shouldn't work on clients in dozens of different sectors. Why? It's inefficient. You can't become an expert in everything. Some sectors are not as profitable as others. Also, you're not suited for every type of business.

Every time you tackle a new industry, you'll have a significant learning curve to understand the industry, its rules and regulations, the competitive landscape, and so on.

That's not to say you should work in just one industry—that would soon get boring, you may run out of potential clients, and you put your business in danger if something happens to that industry. An example of this is the virtual shutdown of the travel and tourism industry during the pandemic.

But eventually, you want to have a coherent client list, at least for your significant clients. You'll probably always have a few clients that fall outside of your focus, and that's fine for variety, but they won't likely be your key clients.

You may consciously decide to focus on an industry category or type of client—e.g., you want to work for fashion clients, and they're the ones you're pursuing—or you may fall into it.

"Falling into it" typically happens if you get a client in a specific industry, then get recommended by that client to a colleague at a similar company or organization. Now you have two clients in the same category. Then, your name gets passed around, and soon you're working for several companies in a vertical, and before you know it, you become an industry expert.

Look around, and you'll find creative services firms that have found a niche to excel in. Some are working mainly on retail, while others focus on packaged goods, government, health care, or sports marketing.

You can define niches however you want. Whatever directions you choose, your goal should be to become an expert in those niches. That allows you to have deeper engagements with your clients and deliver your services more efficiently.

You'll also learn that businesses that are alike generally operate in similar ways, and you can quickly learn their processes and meet their operational requirements.

A case in point: if you have government clients, you'll soon discover they have similar processes for how they do projects. Once you learn them, you'll know what to expect and how to best work with those processes.

Let's say you're doing work for your regional government. You'll find that the national government operates similarly. So, you'll expect RFPs, established hierarchies, long timelines, etc. Once you know how that works, you can adjust your operations to meet these requirements.

Some creative services firms have become very successful by defining their focus by their deliverables rather than client type.

For example, they may focus on supporting sales teams or doing live events like product launches. These firms often work alongside other creative services companies such as ad agencies. Where an ad agency might handle the main advertising for a food account, they will call on the specialty company to take care of the live event product launch.

These can become very profitable niches. Often, there are many steps and communication requirements for each assignment, so by nature, they become large projects.

Knowing these steps, understanding all of the clients' needs, and learning how to manage the projects becomes a real competitive advantage for your firm.

For example, if your agency becomes a "sales support expert," you can approach any company with a sales team, and they will likely listen to your pitch.

So, think about the types of clients or services you want to become known for and concentrate your new business efforts there. Avoid the temptation to say yes to everything and every kind of client.

Having Utilities and Government-Related Accounts Worked for Us

Working as a freelance copywriter, I was introduced to a client at an electrical utility. At the time, their main requirements were brochures for their various electrical conservation programs and newspaper ads. I wrote them for years.

When I formed Fireworks Creative, I brought that client with me. By that time, in addition to their print materials, we were writing, designing, and building their website, creating magazine ads, and producing videos.

Our work with that client brought us other electrical and gas utility clients. They didn't compete with each other, so that wasn't an issue. Moreover, we became known as experts in the sector, and utilities would contact us. That was a massive advantage for us.

At my next company, Context Creative, we continued working for these clients and started working for various provincial government ministries. You can see how these types of clients and the projects they generate are related. That was how we narrowed our focus and became experts in those categories.

We weren't tempted to work with retail clients, fashion, or complicated tech. None of these were our strengths, and people didn't come to us for those anyway.

Key Benefit of Focus—Your Reputation for Industry Expertise

Once you narrow your focus either by client sector or type of deliverable, you'll become known for that. You should promote your expertise on your website, social media, and any other media.

You'll find that your focus generates positive word of mouth. Think of what that means to you. Instead of pitching prospects, they're coming to you. They can quickly see that you understand their requirements and speak their language.

They may even give you a project without competition or having to qualify for it. Your evident expertise has already prequalified you. This allows you to charge more and dictate some of the terms of your engagement.

If they don't come to you, it's much easier for you to approach them with a portfolio of relevant work and a deep understanding of their industry.

To amplify your expertise further, look for opportunities to speak or present at industry events. You want to be the only marketer there, and you'll use your case studies and example of your work throughout your presentation. Then take advantage of networking opportunities to start creating new relationships.

Narrowing Your Focus Doesn't Mean Standing Still

Although you can't be everything to everyone, you do have to evolve with the times. Even if you're a specialist in the latest and greatest, that too will change, and you'll have to move with it.

There will always be tension in how far you can comfortably stretch. Ideally, you want to expand into areas of expertise and client types that build on your current base.

For example, when my companies were creating websites, it made sense also to learn how to create, manage, and deliver email marketing campaigns. Web and email are closely related and required many of the same technologies and skill sets.

So, we learned everything we could about email marketing and sold it as a service to our existing clients and new prospects. We got up to speed quickly and felt confident in what we were offering.

But, sometimes, making the transition into new types of deliverables can go too far. I know of other communications companies that were asked by clients to tackle a product design assignment. Not product marketing, but designing the product itself. Sounds like fun, right? Something outside of the everyday communications assignment.

I don't think it's a good fit. Product design has distinct processes, disciplines, and requirements. It's not something you can learn casually. And, if you're not going to build on it, it becomes a distraction, potentially a costly one.

By nature, creative people like the challenge of the new, of doing something they haven't done before. It feels like it's stretching you, keeping you excited in your work. And indeed, it does all of that.

It's worth having serious and long discussions any time you're thinking of broadening your offerings into new client niches. If you decide to add to your capabilities, you'll need to invest the time to become an expert at your new offering before promoting it to prospects.

Hidden Client Sectors

Many client sectors are obvious. Walk down a shopping street or through a mall, and you'll see a variety of retailers, most of whom advertise. You'll likely have seen some of their advertisements.

Go to a news website, or spend any time on Facebook, and you'll see advertising messages. Open a magazine, and you'll see more ads. Turn on the TV and be bombarded by commercials.

But many sectors are far less evident; in fact, they're hidden from the public. Why? Simply because their messages aren't meant for the general public.

There's a massive market of business-to-business advertising. Some companies advertise to specific industry verticals such as doctors, dentists, lawyers, mining, and manufacturing firms.

You won't see those messages unless you're in the business. But someone is producing all of those websites, photography, charts, illustrations, videos, photography, and social media campaigns.

Take a moment just to focus on health care and the medical industry. Consider the amount of research being done worldwide on genetics, cancer, heart disease, and diabetes. There are studies and breakthroughs in treatment for each of these areas. New equipment is being developed. These advances result in reports, websites, social media campaigns, etc.

Similarly, there is a rich communications market in government or government-related organizations. For every government program, there are detailed reports and communications on what the program has achieved, its further goals, etc.

Generally, these reports can run into hundreds of pages. Sometimes there are specific websites and social media campaigns to promote the reports. They're great projects to have if you qualify for them and know how to tackle them.

Here's an example of this type of project. The Canadian Astronomical Society (CASCA) is a society of professional astronomers devoted to promoting and advancing knowledge of the universe through research and education.

A colleague runs a creative agency that was awarded the project of designing the society's 10-Year Long-Range Report. The report is intended to reach a broad audience, including policy-makers, government agencies, astronomers, and the general public.

This being Canada, the report will be available in English and French versions. The long-form English document runs 180 pages, and the French a bit longer. There are also shorter, summary versions of the full reports.

So, for an organization that relatively few people know exists, here is a hefty project of four reports totaling about 500 pages.

Go onto any federal, regional, or city government website, poke around in the various ministries or departments, and you'll find their initiatives. Look for departments that are in the news like health care, the environment, or infrastructure.

Often, you'll see PDFs of reports that you can download. Take a look at a few of them. Most of them will have been created by creative agencies.

Switching gears, here's a category that likely hasn't crossed your mind: postage stamps. When did you last buy stamps? Years ago? Ever? But every country that maintains a postal service regularly issues new stamps, often every few weeks.

Guess who designs them? Independent graphic designers and design studios. At my last company, we were part of a pool of companies that regularly designed stamps for Canada Post. It's a unique and exciting challenge for designers.

In addition to the stamps, there were collateral items, such as first-day covers, so each stamp became a project with a few components. While you won't get rich designing stamps, these were profitable and unique projects.

I mention astronomical societies and postage stamps only to remind you that it's worth taking the time to look around you to uncover sectors that you hadn't considered.

As a side benefit, you may find there's much less competition there, simply because fewer people know about or qualify for them.

To get at those kinds of projects, you'll likely have to make it onto the organization's vendor list. More on vendor lists coming up.

Secret Criteria for Finding the Best Clients

There is one criterion for working with clients that many creative agencies overlook or never consciously uncover. Not asking yourself one simple question can lead to countless struggles, arguments over the value of your work, and finally, not getting paid what you're worth.

The question you want to answer as early as possible is this: does this company, your prospective client, have a defined budget for the type of work that you do? A related question would be: do they have someone on staff who's in charge of buying and assessing the work you're doing?

Let me explain. When you first meet a prospect, and they start talking about what it is they want from you, you should try to get a sense of who they are and whether there is defined a budget for what you do.

Here are some positive signs to look out for:

- The person you're talking to has the words "marketing," "communications," or "advertising" in their job title.

Their salary is likely being paid by a marketing, communications, or advertising department. Assumedly, they are professionals in that field.

- They come to the meeting with a detailed brief outlining how they see the project. Perhaps they will have emailed this to you in advance to make your time together more efficient.
- They will have a budget and timeline for the project. If this isn't in the brief, they will readily tell you.

Another way to think about your ideal client is that they do what you do but from the client's perspective. You're like two sides of the same coin. For this project, you become a team. You both know how to get this job from initiation to completion, you know what to expect of each other, and you both deliver.

Usually, this type of client also makes sure all the paperwork gets done correctly, so you don't have issues getting paid later.

They'll likely ask you for an estimate, they will approve in writing, and they'll get you a purchase order if you need one. If you need an upfront deposit, they will get that for you quickly so that the project can start.

In short, they are professional clients with budgets dedicated to the type of work you do. Ideally, that is what you want, no matter what industry you're working in. You might not get 100 percent of that, but you should be close.

I can't tell you how much easier it is working for professional rather than amateur clients.

Identifying Amateur Clients

Let's assume you're introduced to a potential client by a friend. You thank your friend for the lead, call up your new prospect, and agree to meet at their office to learn about their business and the project.

The meeting starts well. The client tells you about what they do in general and this project in particular. You notice they don't have a written brief. You ask a few questions along the way and take notes (it would be so much easier if they had a written brief).

From the answers, you realize that this person doesn't usually do projects like this one. They may be evasive about answering some of your questions or give you answers you don't expect.

In the conversation, you may learn that this person is either the company owner or an assistant to the owner. That's the first red flag.

If you're meeting with the owner, it means they don't have anyone in charge of marketing or communications. It's doubtful that the owner has any experience in these types of projects.

You may catch yourself thinking, "Well, it's okay that they don't have much experience in this area. I can educate them along the way." You're trying to be helpful, and you want the job.

During the discussion, you ask about the deadline for the project. Two things to watch for: either a ridiculously tight deadline that you would have no way of meeting, or no real deadline at all, which means the project has low priority and will likely get dragged out for months. Both are red flags that you should note.

Inevitably, at some point in this first meeting, likely reasonably early, they will ask you for a ballpark estimate. "How much do you think this will cost?" That's another red flag.

At this stage, you haven't had time to think about it and work out all the details to provide a comprehensive estimate. It's far too early to quote costs.

Do not, under any circumstance, blurt out a number, not even a ballpark number. If you do, and they agree, you may well regret it, given that you haven't agreed on what's included in the job. In all likelihood, your vision for the project is quite different from theirs.

So, you might respond by asking, "What's your budget for this project?" so that you can come back with a relevant proposal. Can you already guess their answer? Nine times out of ten, they will say something like, "Well, we don't have a budget, but if you give us an estimate, we'll look at it and then decide."

Massive red flag!

Now you have a choice. You could ask a few more questions that you think will help you put together an estimate. Then you'll have to decide how comprehensive you want to make the project.

Is this a $5,000 or $50,000 assignment? It will take you a few hours to write it up and follow through either on the phone or in person.

If you follow this route, consider that you will have invested at least a day or two of your time to meet and come up with an estimate, and you have no idea of their budget. It can be an incredible waste of time.

The Secret Tactic to Get to a Number

You could try one more approach to flush out what they're thinking when it comes to budgets. A former partner of mine was a master at this, which saved everyone a lot of time writing useless estimates that would never get approved.

When he found himself in this type of meeting and realized that the prospect wouldn't give a budget number or range, he would say, "Well, I can't give you an estimate right now on your project because I need to sit down and make sure I include everything you need. However, from what we've been talking about, I can tell you that we've done similar projects for other clients that have ranged from $30,000 to $40,000."

Then he'd watch their face and wait for a reaction. Sometimes it came quickly. "Oh no, that's much more than what we had in mind." And his response, "Well, what were you thinking?" And if they answered, say, $5,000, then he knew that's the number they had coming into the meeting.

Even if they don't say anything, now the "money logjam" has been broken. Now you're talking about money. Depending on how the next few minutes go, you can decide whether you want to provide an estimate and try to work with this client or walk away.

In any case, you shouldn't leave the meeting without a number or a budget range. If they simply refuse to talk about money, it's probably not worth your while to write up an estimate.

Starts Bad, Gets Worse

Despite the red flags along the way, let's say you decide to proceed without any idea of their budget. You may like the person you met with, find the potential job a good fit with your other clients, or simply think that if you can get through this project, there could be a lot more work.

Perhaps along the way, you could train this person or company to become a good client.

Maybe, but I wouldn't bet on it.

What often happens is something like this. You write your first estimate. It comes to $30,000. You follow up to discuss it with them. At this point, it becomes clear that although they like most of what you've outlined, they don't have a $30,000 budget, but rather, $5,000.

After some back and forth where you narrow the project's scope so that it becomes close to a $5,000 job (you're likely fudging the numbers to make them fit), you agree to do the work.

You send them a detailed estimate for the $5,000 project, which you ask them to approve by email, so you have something in writing. Somehow in the hurry to get going, they "forget" to formally approve it, and you don't follow up.

On the estimate, you asked for an upfront deposit (as you should with all new clients). When you bring it up, they say they never pay deposits, and they'll pay you in full when you've completed the job. Against your better judgment, you accept those terms.

Next comes the deadline. They would like the job done by next week. That's totally unrealistic, but they've left everything to the last minute, and now they're counting on you to save them. Once more, you agree to help them out.

To start the job, you need some materials from them that they should readily have, like artwork for logos, any pre-approved legal copy, etc. To work efficiently, you need all of this right away, but it takes them days to get it to you. Now you and your team are working around the clock to make up for their lateness.

In the middle of the project, your new client calls you and, somewhat sheepishly, asks for a favor. Their team just had a meeting, and it seems that in addition to what you're currently doing, they also need a couple of variations of X, Y, and Z. Do you think you could squeeze that in? No extra money, or extra time, of course. And once again, you agree.

Finally, with a lot of sweat, the job is done. At this stage, if you're fortunate, everyone on the client side is happy, and you submit your invoice as agreed upon.

You assume that after everything you've done for them—working at minimum wage if you dared do the math on the hours—you'll at least get paid in a reasonable time. After all, it did say "Net 30 days" on your invoice.

But that probably won't happen.

More likely, someone on the client team will grumble that the job wasn't quite what they expected or that your invoice "got lost" somewhere in accounting. After many phone calls chasing your money, you'll finally get paid five months later. You'll never hear from them again, and you're just as happy not to.

Just to Hammer This Thought Home

Perhaps you think this example was overly dramatic. Actually, just the opposite. I've run into situations similar to this where halfway through a project, someone else on the client side called to say that whoever briefed you was:

1. Wrong
2. Acting on their own without approval
3. Out of his mind
4. Just fired, and they're shutting down the project and won't be paying you

In summary, here is what you're looking for from a client. You might not get everything, but you want most of these points:

1. They have someone on their team dedicated to working with people like you. If it's the company owner, they should give you assurances of the importance of the project to their company.
2. They have defined marketing or communications budgets, just like they have budgets for their rent,

payroll, taxes, etc. Marketing is not an afterthought and doesn't come out of their personal money.

3. They are professionals when discussing the scope of the job, fees, down payments, payment terms, and deadlines. In other words, they understand and respect processes.

4. If they have to provide you with materials to do the job, they get them to you in a timely fashion.

5. They understand that if they ask for additional services, you'll provide them with a further estimate. If it's something small, you may choose to "throw it in," but that's your decision.

6. They will give you a clear understanding of the approval process. You need to know how approvals are handled. It would be nice if everyone in the decision-making process were in the first meeting, but that's rarely the case.

Often there are further internal approvals required (your client's boss, the president, chairman, board of directors) that they will want to make in sequential order. In other words, the board of directors only wants to see it if everyone below them has approved it.

1. If that's the case, they should tell you upfront. Having multiple levels of approval often means you have to make allowances in your estimate for the time it will take for additional presentations and further rounds of revisions.

2. If your client has multiple approval levels, you should strongly suggest that you be the one to present your work up the ladder. You should be there to explain how you got to your solutions and answer any questions they may have.

3. Your client may not allow that to happen. You can ask

and provide all the reasons why it's a good idea, but if they don't let you, there's not much you can do. Just hope that your client can successfully sell up to the higher levels.

Tire Kickers Who Just Waste Your Time

Inevitably, you'll be approached by people who want to talk about doing work for their company. Perhaps they were introduced to you by a friend who thinks you could help them, or they found you through your website or social media.

After a few minutes, you'll start to notice that they're talking in very general terms and asking a lot of questions. It soon dawns on you that in all likelihood, they don't really have a project in mind, nor do they have a budget. To use that colorful phrase, they just want to "pick your brain."

Generally, I'm happy to help out anybody, but after a while, I would get to the point and ask whether there is something specific that our company can do for them. If they say yes, I'll ask them to send me an email with a detailed brief. That alone stops most tire kickers.

This is another case where you'll have to trust your gut instinct on how to proceed. I wouldn't take any more time to write proposals or have further meetings unless I received a satisfactory briefing document. You have to draw boundaries around your time. In this case, if they want something from you, it's only fair that you receive something from them, like a project brief.

Don't Lower Your Prices for Future Promises

If you've been in business for any length of time, you will have heard the come-on of doing something for a low price, or even for free, on the promise of better paying future business.

You already know the answer: No, don't do it. How it starts is how it will continue. There are a few obvious things wrong with this approach.

If someone doesn't have any or adequate budget for the marketing they need to do, they haven't planned for it.

If they have a small budget, you can do a small job, appropriate to the funds available. But don't get sucked into a big production for minimal payment. It sets a precedent. If there are following projects, they'll be sure to ask for the same low rate.

There's also a good chance that there won't be any future business. Either their plans fizzle out and there's no business, or worse, they go to someone else with the bigger projects.

Be Genuinely Interested in Your Clients' Business

The best people in creative agencies are naturally curious. They're interested in everything. Nothing is boring; everything is worth exploring.

That means they get deeply involved in their clients' products and services, their goals and aspirations, their threats and challenges.

When you work for a client, you become part of their team. While you're working for them, you wear the team shirt with the team logo. At least, that's what the client hopes. They want a partner who is "all in"—truly and deeply involved in their business.

Clients can sense it. They also know if you're faking it, just going through the motions, doing the minimal amount of work, and sending the invoice. What can you do to get more deeply involved with your clients? Plenty.

For example:

- You can find and read industry reports that mention your client. Understand what the media says and thinks about your client. What if you learned that surveys show your client's website needs to improve? Is that something you could help them with?
- You can keep track of competitors' websites. What are they writing about? Are they introducing a new product or service? New promotions? Do they have any relevant files to download? Your client plays in a competitive world. You should understand the playing field.
- If you're working in the not-for-profit category, you can look at similar organizations in other regions and countries. How are they tackling some of the same issues? What could you learn from them?
- If your clients are public companies, you can download annual reports and read them. Learn how your client talks to investors and the financial world. Download the competitors' annual reports and study them.
- If they have retail stores or their products are sold in stores, go in and look. Do a store check. How are the displays? Do you have any ideas for how you could improve them?

Why would you do any of this? It's because you're their communications partner.

Whether you're writing, designing, photographing, making films or programming for them, you should aim to know their business as well as they do. You can talk to your clients about your findings and discuss whether they may have an impact on the work you're doing together.

Being deeply entrenched in their business helps make you irreplaceable. You become a true partner. That's what they want, even if they don't come out and tell you. So, cultivate your curiosity and dig in deep.

How Close Do You Get to Your Clients?

I watched a video where a creative agency owner said that he hardly meets with his clients anymore. Everything is done online or by phone.

Working this way is very tempting. It feels more efficient. No time wasted going from your office to theirs. No cost for transportation either. And hey, if you want to get "face-to-face," there's always Skype, Zoom, or other platforms, right?

I think that's a mistake, especially with bigger clients. To be clear, I don't think you should meet in person for every little thing. That's obviously inefficient. At the same time, there are exceptions.

I wrote this book during the pandemic, so Zoom was the popular solution for client meetings. But once we can meet in person again, I think close contact matters.

Face-to-face meetings are the real glue that holds relationships together. Humans are social beings—we have families and friends, throw parties, join organizations and teams, and go out to events to be with other people. There are added layers of connection when we're all in the same room.

If distance is an issue, call your clients. Talking to them creates a much tighter connection than email or Slack.

Having a meeting or a call is a chance to get to know each other better. You'll talk about their kids, pets, sports, upcoming vacations—they become your business friends. Having these kinds of meetings will also help you understand how social they are.

By that, I mean that some clients love to be taken out to lunch once in a while. So, make sure you do that. It's especially appropriate after you've completed a big project together and a celebration is in order. Others won't go to lunch, but they'll be thrilled if you offer to bring coffee and muffins for everyone on the way in to the meeting.

Your goal is to work the way your clients like to work. Each client will be different. Remember, you are in service to your clients. That's what they pay you for.

If you're not the social type—in other words, you'd rather not go to meetings, you feel awkward there, and really can't stand small talk—then you need to find someone for your company who will do this and be good at it.

How often you meet with clients depends on many factors, including their preferences and distance between your offices. But don't let too much time go by between face-to-face meetings.

Here are the times you should ask for an in-person meeting:

- A briefing for a big project. You want to be across the table to ask questions, get feedback, and thoroughly review the requirements. There's a back-and-forth discussion you just won't get any other way. These kinds of meetings often lead to the identification of additional projects. Why would you want to miss that?
- Presentation of concepts. You got the job, and now you have to present your ideas. Don't "mail it in" or try to do it over video conferencing.
- This is your turn on stage to put on a show and sell your thinking. There's chemistry in the room. You need to be there to read it. Sometimes during these kinds of meetings, the "boss," even the company president,

wanders in. They want to know what's new, and you want to be the one to deliver the news.

- Presentation of the final project. You've presented the concepts, they chose one, there were a few rounds of revisions, and now you've got the finished product. The baby has been born! Be there for the presentation, the accolades, the oohs and aahs. Celebrate a little. And again, this is an opportunity to talk about the next project while everyone is excited about this one.

In between these phases, you can do it by phone, email, text, a platform like Slack, whatever they prefer. But never miss out on crucial opportunities to get that much closer to your clients.

The hardest part of the business is getting good clients, ones that are right for you. That's why, once you have them, you need to nurture them.

The more time you spend together, the easier it gets. You understand and trust each other. You have become "partners" to solve the company's communications challenges. Money is rarely a problem. Getting and keeping profitable clients is your ultimate goal.

Remember, if clients don't know you or like you, you're easy to replace. At some point, they'll stop doing business with you.

Getting Even Closer to Your Clients

Storytime: For 13 years, my company Context Creative designed, edited, and produced the guidebook for the IdeaCity conference in Toronto. This three-day conference brings together leading thinkers in the sciences, health, technology, arts, and government. It's the kind of dialogue that makes your brain explode.

We got that assignment because my partner and I attended Idea-City and were blown away by it. One of the speakers, Robert Kennedy Jr., spoke on behalf of a water protection environmental group. He was promoting the cause and trying to raise money.

Afterward, Moses Znaimer, the IdeaCity impresario, said that anyone making a contribution would get an invitation to his private party the next Saturday.

No one seemed to rush the stage. I approached Moses and asked, "How much?" "Five hundred dollars," he said. I said we're in and wrote a check.

That got us to his private party, where we had a chance to get to know each other a bit better. Once he learned what we did, he asked whether we would be interested in designing the book for next year's conference. We said yes. Payment would be money and tickets. And, of course, we would be invited to his insiders' party after that.

We used those tickets to invite clients for a day each at the conference. This was a chance to get them out of the office, away from day-to-day work, and expose them to ideas and speakers they wouldn't usually see.

It was also an opportunity to treat them to a serious expense-account lunch. Now we were sitting next to our clients, chatting about everything except business. The talk revolved around that morning's speakers, vacations, books, movies, family, and so on.

Days like that helped establish a closeness far beyond any work project. It helped us create relationships that would last for years.

The point of this story is that people do business with people they know and trust. The closer you can get to your clients, the more genuinely interested you are, the better. It's helpful if you're naturally gregarious, enjoy meeting and listening to people, and don't mind picking up the check.

How Close Relationships with Clients Paid Off

In all of my agencies, close relationships with key clients paid off year after year. I can think of five people who changed jobs numerous times and each time, took us with them to their new company.

In fact, that is how we got our largest clients, with no pitching or competition. We were simply walked in, introduced as trusted vendors, and started working.

I clearly remember one of our clients leaving her job at a utility to work for another utility. Luckily, we had relationships with others at the first utility, so we continued to work for them.

About a month later, we got a call from our client at her new job. Did we have time to come and see her? Well, of course we did. We assumed we would have to make a presentation of our experience and credentials to this new company, so we prepared an appropriate portfolio.

When we got to the meeting, in addition to our client, there were a few others around the table, including the head of the marketing department.

He said he understood that we had a lot of experience in business-to-business communication programs and that perhaps we could help them. We quickly realized this was not a presentation meeting. It was a project briefing. We never did show our presentation but started taking notes.

That first campaign was well into six figures. It exceeded the client's goals, won numerous awards, and quickly led to a follow-up campaign. From that introduction in 2005, this client relationship is still ongoing and has brought millions of dollars of profitable revenue, numerous awards, and industry credibility.

As I mentioned, I can think of five instances where similar client moves have paid off in this fashion. Being walked in to a new client is so much easier than constant pitching or answering detailed RFPs.

Ask yourself how you can get closer to your clients and become a trusted vendor. Even if you can't meet face-to-face, there are many ways to delight and surprise your clients. Do you know their birthdays? These days, few people send birthday cards. Maybe you could start there.

Another Reason for in-Person Meetings: A Quiet Word on the Side

As wonderful as your agency will be, sooner or later, you or someone on your team will mess up. If you're at a client meeting, they may pull you aside after the meeting to have a little chat about it. If you're lucky, it will be something small that you can quickly compensate for or correct.

But sometimes, you learn that something more significant has happened before the client notices, and you need to talk to them about it.

That's when you want a face-to-face meeting. Yes, it would be more comfortable on the phone (you wouldn't have to look them in the eye while you're talking), and perhaps much easier by email, but that might seem like you're trying to avoid the issue.

Call them and ask for a short meeting. Face up to it in person and make it better.

Another benefit of doing it in person is that potentially you can contain it. Talking it through and coming to a resolution is better for you than a long email chain that could be forwarded and come back to haunt you later.

A Client Insight: Meeting with You is the Most Fun They Have

Have you ever thought of yourself as "the entertainment"? Well, if you are in the creative agency business, you are precisely that.

I'll never forget a client telling me that meeting with us was the most fun they had in their workweek.

We were so creative, we seemed to have so much fun doing our work, our ideas were always better than they expected, they were looking forward to seeing what we had come up with, we had much cooler loft-space offices than theirs—we were the entertainment.

While the rest of their jobs involved pushing paper, working spreadsheets, filing memos, and doing other admin tasks, working together on creative projects lit up their day.

Don't forget that. Make them part of it. Give them credit for their input and their help in creating a successful project. Many of them would like your job or to work at your agency. Invite them to share the glory.

There's Nothing Like Cake

For a time, we were building a lot of websites for clients. These were often months-long projects with many meetings and input from various departments for design, messaging, technology, hosting, maintenance, etc.

When we were finally done, and the site was about to be launched, we always made sure we scheduled a meeting at their office and had a big group in the room to celebrate the project's completion together. And we would surprise them with cake.

Not just any cake. We had a favorite bakery that would make us a big rectangular sheet cake. Covering the whole cake, in icing, was the home page of the new website. When we unveiled it, they laughed and shrieked like kids at a birthday party.

The phones came out to take pictures of the cake before we cut it up. It went out on their social media feeds and internal communications.

People were brought in to admire it. I've met CEOs and Presidents who dropped in to witness the launch of their new site and join us for a piece of cake. There was always enough for everyone in the department.

The cake gave us time to stand around and chat, sometimes with people we didn't otherwise see (e.g., the CEO, president, head of IT). Inevitably, someone would pull one of us aside and already start talking about "the next job" now that we had completed this one.

Cake gets remembered and talked about. It showed that we made the effort to bring some fun into their office, that we thought about them as people, not just clients. There's nothing like a little sugar rush to wrap up a project.

I'm not saying that you should bring or send cake after successful projects... but then again, maybe you should.

Saved the Best for Last—the Key Reason to Meet in Person at their Office

Let's say you're working with a big client. You have one contact there, and you're doing a lot of work for her, but she's just one person in a group of internal marketing people. Her colleagues have projects too, but you're not working for any of them. They have their own suppliers. But, wouldn't you like to work for others in that department? Yes, you would.

Here's where you need to practice diplomacy. Sometimes clients in this position are very protective of you. You are theirs, and they don't necessarily want to share you with the others in their department. They think that if you work for the others too, maybe you won't have enough time for them.

So, don't be too quick to walk around handing out business cards or chatting up the others.

However, if you show up often enough, everyone will begin to recognize you and know that you did the great projects they see around the office.

One day your client will ask whether you have any extra time for one of her colleagues who has a project she might like to discuss with you. Trust me, it will happen.

If everything works out, now you have two clients instead of one. That introduction could easily double or triple your billing with that company.

But you always want to remember your initial client and make plenty of time for her. You can dance with the others, but remember who brought you to the dance.

That's why you want to go to their office for meetings. You want to be available for anyone there who may have projects for you.

Selling Strategy as a Service? Another Reason to Dig in Deep

Many creative agencies also want to include strategy as a separate service they sell. It makes sense because, for many larger campaigns, you need an agreed-upon strategy to do the project, and very rarely does the client bring it to the table. So, it's up to you to create the strategy, get buy-in, and then execute the campaign against that strategy.

But think about it: how can you credibly sell strategy without knowing everything about their business? Why would the client pay you for strategy if you're just skating on the surface?

As a communications supplier, you have to be a quick study and get up to speed in a hurry. You're working with a client who may have years of experience at the company, and now you're in a position of telling them what they should be doing. You had better be confident in your advice.

The only way you're going to get there is to fully immerse yourself in their business. You need to know what the brand stands for, understand the complete brand story and be up to date on their competitors and the markets they operate in. Then you'll have a much better chance at selling strategy, either as a separate project or as part of a larger assignment.

Added Value for Competitive Advantage

When you work with a client for a while, you begin to see opportunities they might not notice. Sometimes it could be related to a specific project; other times, it may be a more general observation. It pays to speak up.

Some, but not necessarily all, of your suggestions will result in more work for you. Whether or not you get the extra work, clients appreciate that you're thinking beyond the specific project for ways to help them.

Let's say you're taking photographs of a new product they're introducing. You could suggest that while you're set up, you could also update the photos for their older products to have fresh images with a consistent look.

Perhaps you're doing headshots for two new staff members. What about updating the portraits of existing staff for the website or other materials so that all the photos are uniform?

Or maybe you're shooting for one particular medium—what about other media? If you're shooting in landscape format, would it make sense also to get images in portrait orientation?

If you're starting a project for a client who also works with other communications partners such as a PR agency, ask your client whether the PR company needs anything that you could accommodate in this job. Extra photos? Video footage?

If you have clients in related fields, perhaps you could introduce them to each other to work together for mutual benefit. For example, if you have two food product clients, could they tag each other in social media campaigns? Perhaps you would create a campaign or images that both could use.

Even if you have just one client in a sector, could you find another company that may want to do a cooperative campaign? Wine and cheese, bread and butter, bacon and eggs—there are many natural pairings.

Adding value to your clients in this way brings you closer to them. They can see that you're always thinking of them. That gives you a competitive advantage and makes it very difficult to replace you.

Enter Awards Shows—Many Clients Love Them

Sometimes it seems like the marketing and communications world runs on awards shows. Many of them, like Cannes, Clio, ADDY, Communication Arts, or Applied Arts, are mostly for people like us who work in design, advertising, illustration, photography, and interactive.

Being chosen and published in their magazines and on their websites is undoubtedly an honor, and your friends and colleagues in the business will send you congratulations.

However, it's worth noting that these shows are strictly beauty contests—the judges are looking solely at the aesthetics. There is no measure of effectiveness or business goals achieved.

Although your peers will likely be very aware of these awards, your clients probably won't be. Strategically, you want to enter shows that make a difference in the business world, the world of your clients.

There are many awards shows, such as the Summit International Awards, where the performance of the piece plays a significant role in the evaluation.

Large industry sectors often have their own sector-specific communication awards shows too. Clients love them—these are their peers, many of whom they'll know.

To enter these shows, you need to include business rationales, metrics, and proof of effectiveness. You'll have to work with your client to get this information. Even the act of collaborating on awards show entries brings you closer together.

These are the shows that many clients value more. Winning here is a combination of aesthetics and business results—and is as much recognition for the client as it is for the creators.

The other benefit of these shows is that there tend to be many categories, which gives you many ways to enter, and a greater likelihood of winning.

Entering these awards takes time and involves entry fees (awards shows are big business). Who pays the fees? You do. It's the cost of business and helps cement your relationship.

A tip for awards shows: if you win, you'll get a plaque or some sort of trophy. If you want one for your client and another for yourself, you'll have to pay for the second one. Do it. Your client will certainly want one, and you should have your own trophy shelf.

In our early days, we thought that entering these shows was a waste of time and money. Just vanity, right? Wrong. If you're doing effective work for clients, talk to them about entering it in select shows. Your client might be familiar with shows that they've entered before. Be sure to consider them.

If you win any awards, make some noise on your social media and website. And, of course, give lots of credit to your clients!

One Secret for Landing Big Clients

Some creative agencies wonder why it's so hard to get work for big clients such as car companies, banks, beverage and alcohol companies, and various levels of government. They try calling or emailing to get appointments, they drop off portfolios, but don't get anywhere.

The answer is quite simple: most of these organizations have preferred vendor lists. These lists are suppliers that they have prequalified for their marketing and communications staff.

When someone in their marketing department wants to initiate a project, they refer to the company's lists and find one or more vendors that would be a good fit for that particular job. Depending on the organization and the size of the project, they may call a few companies on the list to submit proposals.

If your agency isn't on the list, you obviously won't get called. Generally, the marketing people aren't allowed to use anyone who is not on the list. But sometimes there are exceptions. Read on...

How to Get on a Preferred Vendor List

If you want to work for these companies or organizations, your first task is to determine whether or not they have such a list, and if they do, whether there is more than one list. Some companies maintain multiple lists (by types of work, by size of vendor), so it's essential to get on the right one.

As a quick example, when we wanted to get on a provincial government list, we first pursued getting on the ad agency list. But according to their criteria for ad agencies, we weren't big enough and didn't offer some of the mandatory services.

However, they also had a design studio list, which we applied for when it opened up. We made it onto that list.

There's no magic way to find out whether a company maintains a preferred vendor list. You'll have to dig and do some research. If you know someone who does work for one of these companies, you could ask them. Or better yet, if you know someone at the company or organization, ask them.

Or do an online search. For example, try searching "doing business with [name of company or organization]." Once you establish that a company/organization has such a list, you need to identify the person who controls it. They'll have someone who's in charge of "vendor services" or some such title.

Ultimately, you want to find out how often they open up the list for new submissions, when they'll open it next, and what's involved in the submission process. Typically, large organizations only open up the list every few years, so this requires patience.

If you make it to the point where you are applying to be on the list, be prepared to complete a very detailed submission. The questions and requirements often go on for many pages, so it will take some work to get your proposal together. Leave yourself plenty of time.

Lastly, follow the rules. Likely they will only give you one opportunity to ask any questions about the application, so be sure to read it thoroughly and submit your questions. Sometimes companies will do this on a conference call, other times by email. Usually, afterward, you'll get answers to all questions asked, not just yours.

There will be a deadline for your submission. Companies are very strict about these deadlines, so if it says March 1, 12:00 p.m., then you'll be refused at 12:01.

Usually, you have to deliver your package to a specific person, and you'll get a time-stamped receipt as proof of your delivery. Generally, my companies delivered our packages in person. Sometimes we used couriers, making sure they knew that timing was critical.

It will take many, many hours to complete this type of submission. Don't blow it at the last minute by being late.

Vendor List Questions to Watch For

You should be able to answer most questions on the vendor submission form reasonably quickly. But one area that you may want clarification on revolves around various types of insurance. Up to this point, you may not have liability or cyber insurance if none of your clients have asked for it.

Vendors may ask for $5 million or more in various types of insurance. That means you have to find an insurance broker who will provide it (not all do) and pay for it out of your pocket.

If you don't have that type of insurance, or don't have enough coverage, you'll want to clarify whether you can promise to get it if you make it onto the list. In most cases, that should be acceptable. If you do get on the list, you'll have to get the insurance and show proof of your coverage.

A Tip on Your Portfolio with the Vendor Submission

The vendor application may also ask for a portfolio in PDF form. If you are accepted, your submission, including your portfolio PDF, will go into a database, and the organization's internal staff will refer to it when they're looking to choose a vendor for an assignment.

Knowing that staff will look at it on a monitor, my companies formatted our portfolio in landscape orientation to match the screens. We also customized our portfolio for each submission with work that was relevant to the potential client. Don't get lazy and submit the same generic portfolio every time.

Ahead of the actual portfolio samples, we would include pages such as a brief company profile, how we work, and our approach to integrated communications. We created a series of message pages that allowed us to insert the ones we thought were appropriate for a particular submission.

These pages helped individuals in the organization get to know us a bit. Remember, you usually don't have the opportunity to make in-person presentations, and you don't know who will be looking at your portfolio, so it's worth adding information about your company in addition to the work samples.

Each case study page also included information such as a description of the project, project scope, results, and any awards won.

For example, for an annual report, the text would say:

- Ministry of Finance—Digital Annual Report (60-70 words of description)

- Project Scope (60-70 words outlining the scope)
- Results (how the piece was used, distributed, recognized in awards shows, etc.)
- Shown Here (cover, introductory pages, financial reporting pages)

Of course, you can create your portfolio pages however you see fit, but we believed in providing detail for those who chose to read them. It gave each page a professional, thoughtful look.

Getting on the List Doesn't Guarantee Business

A few weeks after the submission date, they will notify you whether you made it onto the list. If you were accepted, congratulations. You're one step closer to a new client, but with no guarantees.

Now, your submission goes into the database, and the organization's internal communications staff will refer to that when they're looking for vendors. But in the meantime, they don't want you calling them to make presentations or pitch for work. You just have to wait until they call you.

That's why it's critical to have a presentation that will catch their eye when they're going through the database.

Once you get your first job from one of these clients, you have to work very hard to establish a relationship with the person or group you're working with. This project is your foot in the door. You want them to call you for their next project, and you want others in the department to become aware of you. That may take some time but can result in a steady flow of significant projects.

For This Type of Client, Personal Contact is More Important Than Ever

Vendor lists act as gates to keep people out. That's good for you if you're on the inside. It means the competition is limited to those who made it onto the list, rather than every competitor out there.

However, even if you've done a project for one of the marketing people, you don't have a license to call them and ask about other projects. They are usually strict about keeping vendors at arm's length.

That's why it's so essential to build rapport during your project. Without going overboard, try to have face-to-face meetings rather than only email or phone for presentations, briefings, and getting revisions. You need to build that relationship in the time that you're working together.

Also, by their very nature, these are large organizations. So, what typically happens is that you'll go to a meeting where they will have a few people present in addition to your client contact.

Who are these people? They may be other internal clients involved in the project you're working on, project managers, or coordinators. Pay attention to them. Try to get cards and figure out who they are.

Chances are, they work with many internal clients, and they will talk about you to them. This was one way we grew within our clients. We would get invited to pitch projects with new internal clients because we were recommended by one of these people in the room.

Can You Get Around the Vendor Lists? Maybe…

Here is where having a deep network pays. Let's say you were working for a client, and you had a tight relationship with one person there. You did many projects together, and you'd love to work with her forever.

Then one day, she tells you she's leaving her job and going to work for a large company or the government, where, of course, they have vendor lists. Most likely, you're not on any of those lists. Now what?

First, hopefully you have developed a network of relationships within the company that your client is leaving. You'll want to find out who is taking your client's place and introduce yourself to maintain that business. If you don't do that, you may have lost an important client when your contact moves.

Then, have a coffee with your ex-client to congratulate her on the new job and ask a few questions. You'll want to find out whether there's an opportunity to work together, and about their vendor lists and how they're defined to determine which list you should apply for, and when they're next open for new applicants.

One of your questions should be whether there is a dollar threshold below which they can work with anyone they choose while you're waiting for the list to open so that you can apply.

In my experience, some organizations with vendor lists would let their staff choose anyone they wanted on projects where the total billing would be under $25,000 or some similar number.

Find out whether this is the case and whether they would consider you for any suitable projects where the budget will be below the threshold.

In the past, I've had clients in this situation invite us for smaller projects before we got onto the list. In some cases, they would even break up larger projects into distinct deliverables, each of which was under $25,000 (shhh!).

If you start to work this way, you still won't be on the vendor list. You won't qualify for larger projects that can't be broken up, and you won't likely be working for anyone else but your contact. But at least you're on the inside with a new client while you wait to get onto the list.

Chapter Takeaways

- It's critical for you to find the right clients for your company and then develop long-term relationships with them. How you work with your clients will often determine how long you will maintain that relationship.
- A narrow focus helps you develop industry expertise that fuels your reputation. That makes it much easier to get new clients.
- Go after "professional clients." Try to avoid the amateurs. They're hard work and rarely profitable.
- It is far better to have ongoing, profitable work with a smaller group of clients than to always be chasing new ones to replace those you've lost. Getting new clients that are right for you is the hardest part of the business.
- You want to become their trusted partner, one that they look forward to working with on project after project.
- Personal relationships are the key to long-term clients. People work with people they know and like. Whatever it takes—coffee, cake, lunch, awards shows—is worth it to deepen your relationship.
- If you want to work with larger companies and organizations, you'll probably come up against vendor lists. It will take some detective work to figure out how to get onto the appropriate lists.
- Being on a vendor list works for you by keeping much of the competition out.

15

MANAGING YOUR AGENCY'S GROWTH

"I love to be a graphic designer, but could we get rid of clients somehow please?"

— Erik Spiekermann

Are You Getting the Right Client Mix for Your Agency?

When you're first starting an agency, you're probably not thinking about managing growth or your client mix. Whether you're working solo or in a small group, you're looking for business to keep your company going. You're mostly thinking about building a client roster, ideally steady clients.

Assuming you see some success and you have a few clients, you have to start thinking more carefully about the kinds of clients you actually want. You can look at this in several ways.

Let's say you're a design studio. What types of clients are you looking for? In your business plan, if you wrote one, you should have outlined who you see as ideal clients. If you didn't make your ideal client list, now is the time to do it. "Anyone with money" is not the right answer.

For example, some studios focus on packaging, so they're looking for clients that need packaging designs or revisions. By nature, they don't design websites.

Or maybe you're a design and strategy consultancy with a focus on not-for-profit organizations.

Perhaps you're a web developer, so you don't care so much about the type of business, but your focus is on websites and surrounding technology. In other words, you're not going to design a brochure or print ad.

However, it's easy to get led astray. People will come to you, asking you to do projects that don't fit your company. It can be tempting to say yes, especially if you're not that busy, the budget seems to be fair, and with a bit of stretching, you think you could do it.

Here are the problems with saying yes to projects that are outside of your niche or capabilities:

- These projects take away time from pursuing your ideal types of clients.
- You're not going to build on this. Whatever you create will not likely end up in your portfolio since it's not a direction you want to pursue.
- There's also a chance you won't complete the project. That means not getting paid, wasting time, and being miserable.

It pays to have a firm understanding of your ideal client mix, so you can dedicate your time targeting those clients and making them aware of your services. So, if you haven't yet made a list of ideal clients for your company, do it now.

Is Your Growth Profitable?

As you run your company, you'll have a general idea of whether it's profitable. Can you pay your bills? Are you saving money for your financial cushion? Are you personally making enough money? Does your accountant think you're meeting expected levels of profitability?

Let's assume for now that the answer is yes to everything.

However, do you know which clients are more profitable than others? It's an interesting exercise to analyze your projects and look at profitability per project and client.

To do this, you need to look at your estimates and invoices for a project, and then your corresponding time sheet information (this is one reason you want accurate time sheets). How close were you in your actual deliverable to what you estimated and billed?

Do a few typical projects per client and then by project type, and you'll start to see how accurately you're estimating and billing.

Once you've done that, you'll have to figure out what to do about it. That all depends on your findings. Are you doing the right types of projects? Do you have the right talent working on the projects? Maybe there's a flaw in your estimating. You won't know until you go through the exercise.

Gathering this information is something either a project manager or a financial person could do. Then you have to analyze the data and come to some conclusions.

You will likely find that some clients or some types of projects are more profitable than the rest. That may guide you in the kinds of projects and clients you're looking for to grow your agency.

The main takeaway here is that although you may be anxious for more new business, you really should only focus on new business that has a high probability of being profitable for you.

Sure, you could do favors for friends or take on one or two projects that don't fit your ideal client profile, but you should have a relentless focus on finding the right types of clients and projects for you.

Here's a quick example. At Context Creative, we worked for the provincial government. For some studios, this type of client isn't easy. First, there's the challenge of getting onto the vendor list, and once you're there, you'll have to contend with a substantial amount of detailed paperwork and client hierarchies. That alone causes many studios to shy away.

But we figured it out and were able to handle it, turning out good projects that led to more of the same. All of them were profitable. We actively pursued this type of business, and it became a significant portion of our revenue.

Is One Client Taking Up Too Much of Your Time?

When you're starting, you'll likely have a lot of little clients. But, there's a good chance you'll also have one or two big clients. These clients give you project after project—they're happy with your work, and you're thrilled with the ongoing assignments. You're making good money, maybe winning some awards, and the samples look great in your portfolio.

They may have been the reason you started your company in the first place. That's how I launched my first company—a few smaller clients and one big one.

However, if you're not careful, that can become a dangerous trap. What if your contact at the big client leaves for another job, someone new comes in, and they have their own network of suppliers?

Or all of a sudden, their budgets dry up? They're no longer supporting the programs that kept you so busy. I've been there, and it's not a nice feeling. In that type of situation, you are very vulnerable.

As a rule of thumb, you should not have one client account for more than 25 percent of your billing or two clients give you more than 50 percent of your billing.

The answer, of course, is to ramp up your new client acquisitions. By adding profitable new clients, you're reducing your dependency on one or two big ones.

I know it's easier said than done, but if you're in that position, you need to make it a top priority to diversify by bringing on more clients.

Review your billing over the past year. Break it down by client. If you have one client responsible for more than 25 percent or two for more than 50 percent of your billing, you're in a danger zone that you need to get out of—the sooner, the better.

How Many Clients Should You Have? Not Too Many

Have you ever wondered what the ideal number of clients would be for your agency? Let's assume these are steady clients for whom you do several projects throughout the year. Although the clients range in size, they all have ongoing assignments for you.

I'll propose a simple answer for you. Aim for about ten. If you had ten substantial clients for whom you did consistently profitable assignments, you'd have a good company.

With ten clients, you and your team could become experts in their businesses so that you can provide strategies and creative with real impact to help them achieve their goals.

In addition to that core ten, you'll likely have a few projects going through your shop that may, in the future, turn into steady client work, but for now, they are just one-off projects. That's okay; they don't count as one of your ten.

Ideally, of those ten, none are more than 25 percent of your billing.

Things to consider about the ten-client rule:

- Although you may not be aware of it at the time, at any given moment, you're probably in the process of losing a client. There may be changes at the client (people have moved on, they've lost their budgets, the company got bought, etc.), or you're just not seeing eye to eye, which means that soon, you won't be working together. That's why you should always be looking for new business to maintain your ten clients.
- The ten-client rule works whether you're a small or big agency. Small agencies will likely have ten smaller clients. Big ones will have bigger clients.
- You may think you want many more than ten clients. I would suggest you focus first on getting ten substantial clients, rather than a rag-tag bunch of smaller ones. Each client comes with a learning curve, and each will take a certain amount of admin time. Make sure you have a core group of worthwhile clients.
- If you have fewer than ten good clients, you may be vulnerable. Let's say you have six clients. What would happen if your best client leaves? That would likely be a big hit for your company. Pick up the pace of your new business efforts to get ten.

Look for Growth Within Your Niches

When you're looking for new business, the first place to look is within your existing niches.

In most cases, you can't take on direct competitors in the same region who are going after the same customers. But some of your clients may operate only within a specific region, so that you could look for similar companies outside of that area.

You should consider businesses that work with each other in the same industry. One may be a supplier to the others, or work in partnership with them. If you already know how some of the industry companies operate, you'll have a short learning curve for others.

For example, you may have a client that manufactures office chairs. It's a small leap to approach companies making office tables, furniture systems, and filing components. They're all in the same industry but not competing with each other.

How can you find some of these companies? Many industries have associations. See whether they have a directory that lists the members and explore from there. They'll likely also have industry websites or publications. Of course, search engines work too.

In my last company, the big niches were electric utilities, health care, and government ministries. In every case, we started with one client and grew from there.

Often it was because one of our contacts changed jobs from one company to another in the same sector and took us with them. Or we were on the vendor list, and word of our work with one client on the list got around to others.

New Business Goal: Make Your Next Client Your Biggest One

Let's assume you're actively looking for new business (you should be). Why not target a client that has the potential to become your biggest client? If your current largest account is billing $150,000 a year, try to identify a potential client that would bill $250,000 a year or more with you. That's the way to accelerate growth.

I see too many creative agencies aiming too low by going after small accounts. Perhaps it's a lack of self-confidence or their existing networks. Make a concerted effort to keep ratcheting up.

The 80/20 Rule Always Exerts Its Force—Fight Back

You can apply the 80/20 Rule to at least two aspects of the creative agency business:

- 80 percent of your billing or profits will come from 20 percent of your clients
- 80 percent of your problems will come from 20 percent of your clients (not the same 20 percent)

You need to fight against both of these. You don't want 80 percent of either billing or profit to come from just 20 percent of your clients. That puts you in a dangerous position.

To keep the math simple, if you have 10 clients, you don't want 80 percent of your billing to come from two of them. So, you have to add bigger clients to spread out your sources of revenue. Remember, ideally no more than 25 percent of your billing from any one client or 50 percent from any two.

As for problems, you don't want to spread them around, but rather to eliminate them. If you find most of your problems come from a few clients, you need to take steps to fix them.

The irony is that generally, it's not your biggest, most profitable clients that are giving you problems. It's often the smaller ones, perhaps ones that don't belong on your client list.

Either fix the problems or get rid of the troublesome clients. I know, easier said than done, and revenue is revenue. But you can't let problems fester. Make a decision and do something about it.

Should You Ever Fire a Client? Yes

Some clients aren't worth the money they pay you. These aren't the kinds of clients you want to keep. Why would you fire a client? There are many reasons. Here are three:

1. They are consistently unprofitable for you. They demand more than they're willing to pay for and have ongoing disagreements with you about fees. The easiest way to part company is to raise the fees in your estimates. They may try to negotiate the estimates down. Stand your ground, and they'll soon leave.
2. They're abusive either to one of your staff or all of you. If it's a junior person on your client's team, and you can talk to someone there to correct this, then, by all means, try this first. But if it's a senior person, it's time to act. Make sure they've paid their invoices, and then just fire them. You will be relieved the minute you do this. An abusive client drags everyone down. Don't put up with it.
3. You've outgrown them. Sometimes you'll have a small client that you've had forever. Back when you first started working together, you charged much less than you do now. If you're on good terms with them, tell them you have to raise your rates. You may even recommend smaller creative agencies that would be a better fit for them.

How do you know whether you should fire a client? It's simple. If it crosses your mind, if you think you'd be better off without them, you're already on the path. If you keep thinking about it, it's probably time to do it. Get it over with, and move on.

Above All, Meet Your Deadlines

As your company grows, you'll find yourself juggling jobs. You'll be in the middle of a big project when you get a call from another client (or even the same one) to take on a few more assignments. You have to be careful here in the promises you make to the clients about when you can deliver.

It's far better to tell them upfront that you can take on their project, but you'll only be able to start on date X, and you could have it finished by date Y than to say you can start right away and then call at the last minute to tell them you need more time.

If there's one thing clients hate, it's an unreliable supplier.

Remember the survey about what clients value most? Reliability is easily number one. When you promise to deliver next Wednesday, your client may have set up an internal meeting for Thursday to show your work to her boss. If you delay your delivery at the last minute, you've embarrassed her. It's the fastest way to lose a client.

Meet your deadlines, be five minutes early for in-person client meetings, and deliver on your promises. Don't be a "flakey artiste." You're running a business, and people are counting on you.

The Good, the Bad, and the Ugly of RFPs

A Request For Proposal (RFP) is prevalent in the world of large corporations and government. In theory, it's a fair way for them to get competitive bids for projects.

In some cases, organizations simply post RFPs on their websites and allow anyone who feels qualified to answer. Other times, the organization invites a selected list to respond to an RFP.

Answering an RFP can be your opportunity to gain a new client or at least win a significant project. They are typically issued for large projects, so it may be worth your while to respond. However, before you jump in, you should know that answering an RFP will chew up many hours.

If you start answering RFPs, you'll soon find that there are at least two types. Some have a prequalifying phase where they are just looking for your credentials to determine whether you'll get invited to respond to the proposal for the actual project. This phase is mostly standard questions that you should be able to answer quickly if you decide to go ahead with it.

Other RFPs combine the prequalifying phase with the project outline. Here, they will ask for a detailed estimate on the project. They'll usually provide you with information on how they score responses.

It can be telling to see how heavily they weigh the lowest cost in their evaluation. We tended to avoid answering RFPs that were strictly based on price.

Before you think about responding to an RFP, you'll want to consider whether you seriously stand a chance to win it. You should be aware that most organizations put out RFPs because they are obligated to work that way, either by law or internal culture.

But in some cases, they already know which supplier they're going to choose, and the rest of the respondents don't stand a chance. That can be hard to determine if you don't have any inside information.

Sometimes RFPs are written for a specific supplier to win. For example, they may reference a particular technology used by one supplier or ask for experience or deliverables that only one company offers.

On the other hand, maybe you're the company with the inside track. You've done work for this organization, they're happy with you, but you have to go through the RFP process to get this next project. A word of caution: don't take it for granted that the project is yours. You still have to give it your best response and assume you're in a competition.

My take on RFPs is that I wouldn't go after an open RFP if my company had no prior relationship with the organization. In all likelihood, it's a waste of time.

Even if we were invited to answer, we would weigh our odds of winning before responding.

Did we know anyone at the organization? Was there a good reason we were on the list, or are they just filling a list because they have to? How many are on the list? Did we have a 1 in 3 chance of winning, or was it 1 in 15?

Did it seem like they had already chosen their winner, and this was just a formality? Was this a one-time project or an opportunity to get a new client with ongoing work?

And just to make it more confusing, sometimes we felt like we had to answer an RFP even if we didn't think we'd win this one so that we would get invited to the next one that could be ours.

From an organization's perspective, seeing your RFP response may be their way of getting to know you. If you don't respond, you may never get invited again.

Whether or not you answer and how you answer is up to you. If this is something you want to pursue, just know that you'll get better at it with practice. Most RFPs have standard sections that you'll be able to complete quickly. But there will be parts that you'll need to create from scratch, which will take time.

Some organizations will allow you to ask questions afterward if you didn't win. We usually participated in that. You may learn a few things to improve your next responses. I think it's worth talking with them on the phone if you have the opportunity. It's generally just a few minutes.

We were selective in which RFPs we answered, and we won our fair share.

Don't Want to Answer RFPs Ever? Your Choice

I know some creative agencies have a policy of never answering RFPs, even if they're specifically invited. There's a sense they're insulted that they have to compete and weren't just awarded the project. To that, I say, fine—one less competitor.

Yes, RFPs take a lot of time and work, but generally, they're for big projects. And once you've answered a few of them, they get much more straightforward.

You'll also get better at figuring out whether you have a good chance of winning before deciding whether to participate.

More and more, organizations are working with RFPs, so if you don't want to respond to them, you have no chance of working with that company. Think about it.

RFPs and Spec Work

Years ago, advertisers would routinely ask for speculative work as part of a pitch for their business. Advertising agencies and other creative suppliers would spend small fortunes creating fully developed campaigns for nothing (FREE, can you believe it?) in hopes of winning the business.

Fortunately, the industry woke up one day and came to its senses. These requests were unethical and exploitive. Industry groups and associations came together to denounce the practice, and members of these groups put an end to it.

Now and then, you'll get a client asking you to develop some spec work as part of an RFP. Generally, if you point them to the industry's stance on the practice, they back off with a thousand apologies and take the spec work off the requirement.

However, some clients still have ways of getting around this. They'll offer everyone answering the RFP a small amount, say $5,000, knowing that the contestants will each end up putting in $25,000 worth of work to showcase their brilliance. It borders on unethical but stays within the guidelines.

If you're faced with this kind of offer, you'll have to decide. I would still look at it the same way: do you know anyone at the client, do you know why you're on the list, do you think you stand a reasonable chance of winning?

Chapter Takeaways

- Find the right clients for your business. Figure out how to get the clients you want. Ideally, they have budgets for what they want to do, they're professional in their dealings with you, and they pay.
- Aim for ten good steady clients. That's a base for any

creative agency.

- Keep your eye on the finances. Make sure your growth is profitable.
- No single client should be more than 25 percent of billings. No two clients should be more than 50 percent. Pay attention to this.
- Fire abusive clients. They're a drain on you and your business.
- Decide whether or not you want to answer RFPs. If you do, be strategic about it. Answer only the ones where you think you have a fair shot at winning.

16

TALKING TO CLIENTS ABOUT MONEY

"If you want to know what God thinks of money, just look at the people He gave it to."

— Dorothy Parker

Get Comfortable Talking About Your Fees

If you're currently working freelance, you're already talking about money when you give clients estimates and invoices.

However, if you take a close look at your billing and the time you spent on your projects, you may conclude that you haven't been charging enough. That is often the case. Why? It likely has to do with your attitude about money.

Many people look at the freelance income as "extra money," something that supplements their income. As a result, they spend too much time for what they're charging or calculate their estimates at an unrealistically low rate. After all, since freelance money feels like a bonus on top of your regular salary, it doesn't matter that much.

But once you depend on that money as the sole source of income, that kind of thinking is dangerous.

People get funny about money. You may have heard:

"Mo' money, mo' problems."

"Money doesn't buy happiness."

"Money is the root of all evil."

"I just need enough money to live on."

How you think and talk about money will be very important if you're trying to run your agency.

If you shy away from money, if you're uncomfortable talking about it, you will likely be undercharging for your services. If you wish you could just do the creative work and not have to talk about the fees, you have an unhealthy relationship with money. That has to change.

For example, if you are challenged on an estimate and immediately back down and offer to reduce it, you're playing a losing game. You're doing that because you don't want to discuss money, and you hope that by reducing the amount, you no longer have to talk about it. Right?

You need to be at ease with money conversations. You'll want to find diplomatic ways to explain your estimates and invoices so that clients understand, agree, and pay you what you're asking.

Ideally, you should be unemotional but comfortable talking about the money. It's merely a form of exchange so that projects can get done. Clients need to feel that it's a fair exchange. You should be ready to discuss and support your estimates and invoices in a way that makes sense to the client.

Just remember that clients have choices. If you're uncomfortable talking about money, someone else who isn't will end up getting the job.

In some cases, you may have to explain your processes and how you work so that clients understand how you got to the dollar amounts. We always did that in our estimates, which were quite detailed and outlined our thinking.

We wanted our estimates to leave the prospective client with the feeling that we were thorough, we had worked through processes that create successful projects, and that our fees were reasonable for the amount of work involved.

Talking About Money. Yes, Let's Talk

Many people have been brought up not to talk about money. When was the last time you asked someone straight out, "How much do you make?" Probably never, right?

Yet, once you're in business, you frequently have to talk about money. Even if you're working with professional clients who have budgets allocated for the work that you do, you may still come up against uncomfortable money situations.

Here's an example: let's say a long-term client briefs you on a project and gives you a budget of $10,000. At first glance, the budget seems reasonable for the scope of the project.

But once you go back and review the brief and then create a detailed breakdown, you realize that to include all of the deliverables requires a budget of $15,000 at the rates you've been charging. That's a significant difference.

Your first step should be to reexamine the brief to make sure you didn't misinterpret it. Ideally, you'd like to be able to deliver the project within the client's stated budget, but most importantly, you also need to make a profit.

After you've reviewed the brief and your estimate again and determined you've answered it correctly, you have a few choices. Two of them mean you have to talk to the client about money. What should you do?

Your first option is to do the job for $10,000. You might convince yourself that if you're efficient, you'll still make a profit and that avoids talking about it with the client. Just do the job as if the budget was adequate.

Or you can call the client and say you need another $5,000 to do the project. They might not be happy to hear that if it's put to them that bluntly. It may feel confrontational.

Another option is to meet with the client to sit together and review the brief and your estimate. You want to show the client how you got to your estimate to meet the brief.

Your goal for this meeting is one of three outcomes:

1. Agree to reduce the number of deliverables to make it a $10,000 project.
2. Explore whether the client can find another $5,000 to complete the project as defined.
3. Or agree to break the project down into phases where you can deliver a $10,000 phase now with the rest to be completed at a later date with an additional budget.

If you agree to reduce the project, and if the difference is significant, you should look for ways to cut a big chunk off the project rather than nibble away a bit at each section. If you do the latter, you'll find that you end up doing the whole project, but for $10,000.

On the other hand, if the difference is 10 percent of the whole project or less, it may make sense to look for ways to shave off smaller aspects of the deliverables.

Having these types of money conversations requires confidence and the ability to talk about dollars and cents in a straightforward way. This is not the time to get emotional. It's not personal, and no one is trying to rip anyone off—it's just business. It's in everyone's interest to find an equitable solution.

But, in a gentle, firm way, you have to make sure you're working to make a profit.

When Not to Talk About Money

There are indeed times when you don't want to talk about money —at least, not too specifically. Here are a couple:

Scenario 1

The client calls you up and gives you the outline of a project on the phone, and asks, "How much?"

Don't answer. Even if you ask a few more questions to get additional details about the job, it's still not a proper briefing, and you haven't sat down to create an appropriate estimate. Your answer should be, "Let me quickly pull together an estimate for you just to make sure I've covered all the deliverables. I can get that for you by tomorrow."

When the client has had a chance to review the estimate, they might change or add to some of the deliverables, which means you'll have to revise it anyway.

Scenario 2

The client asks whether you can do a project that is very similar to a project you did last month but with just a few little changes. They ask, "Do you think you can do it for the same budget?"

Once again, don't answer the question directly. Your answer should be something like, "Can you send me an email with a bit more detail, and I'll review the previous project. I can get an estimate back to you quickly."

So, two things have to happen here. You want the client to detail whatever makes this different from the last project, and you want to review that previous job to refamiliarize yourself with it and determine whether you made any money on it.

Once you get the details from the client, you can create a new estimate in writing for the client to approve.

In short, you never want to give a verbal estimate, especially to a verbal briefing. Ideally, you get everything in writing, and certainly, you give everything to the client in writing.

What about the Time Spent on Project Meetings? Who Pays for That?

Your clients do. If you ever get asked by amateur clients—no professional client would ask this—"Do you charge for meetings?", the short answer is yes, you charge for meetings. It's part of working together.

Look at it this way: when you're in a meeting with a client, are they getting paid for their time? Of course they are. It's part of their job to meet with you. So why wouldn't you get paid?

The longer answer goes something like this, "We provide you with detailed estimates that take into account everything we put into the project. That includes the time and effort for client consultations which we know from experience are critical to the success of any project."

To smooth the way to get paid for meetings, be sure to use the right words in your estimates and communications. For example, it's not a "meeting," it's a "working session," a "client consultation," or "strategy planning session." Our estimates always had line items for working sessions. There was never any dispute about them.

Chapter Takeaways

- You need to be able to talk to clients about money without getting emotional or confrontational. It's just business.
- Do everything in writing so that the details and the dollars of the estimate are clear. Don't feel pressured to give an estimate on a phone call.
- Make sure the budget meets the job requirements. Break down any bigger projects to ensure you know how you're doing it and getting paid for all the steps along the way.
- And yes, you charge for meetings. But call them working sessions.

17

YOUR ESTIMATES CAN MAKE OR BREAK YOU

"Learning new systems and processes is not mandatory... but neither is staying in business"

— Bobby Darnell

There Are a Few Ways to Estimate

For creative agencies, there are generally three ways to estimate and bill:

1. By the hour
2. By defined deliverable
3. By retainer agreement

Most creators choose one and apply it to the majority of their projects. However, you can mix and match depending on the type of project and client preferences.

In my experience, we estimated and billed by deliverable. That type of transaction is most familiar to people. Think about how you buy any product. You buy apples, a shirt, a meal in a restaurant—you know what you're getting and how much it will cost.

You don't care how many hours went into it, and you're not buying it on a monthly retainer basis. (Although companies are trying many versions of retainer-style transactions, where for example, you get a box of vegetables delivered once a week. Any subscription-based arrangement is essentially a retainer.)

This next section covers what I think is critical if you're billing by deliverable. Further on, you'll find a few pages on billing by retainer. It's worth exploring and learning more to see whether you can make the retainer model work for you. We didn't use it, but if I were starting another agency today, I would investigate it at length to try to make it work, at least for some clients.

Estimates are a Secret to Business Success

It's hard to overstate how critical detailed estimates can be to your success. Well-written estimates build client confidence. They are a way for clients to see how you're going to work before you start. In a competitive situation, a thorough estimate will help you win the project because the client will better understand what you're proposing.

Detailed estimates will also help you complete projects successfully because they act as checklists. Both you and the client can check off the steps you've taken. The better you describe your project, the lesser the chance of scope creep. A detailed estimate means if it's not included in the document, it's not in the budget.

Finally, estimates form the basis of your invoices, which will help client accounting departments approve your payment.

If you think about it, how you do your estimates is a good indication of how you run your company. Remember that the first thing a new client will see from you will be your estimate on that initial project. It may determine whether you get the work or any following jobs.

Written Estimates for Everything

You shouldn't do any project, no matter how small, without a written estimate. While you may think you could ballpark a project on the phone without writing anything down, you'll inevitably miss details that will cost you.

A written estimate means you've captured all the project details, and you're getting written confirmation to proceed. It also allows the client to review. Sometimes, during this review, clients find additional items to include, and the job grows.

When it comes time to invoice, you're going to refer to your estimate to create the invoice.

"Estimate" vs. "Quote"

Let's take a moment to talk about language. Always call it an "estimate," not a "quote."

Estimate means it's your best assessment of what you will charge based on what you've described in the document. If there are any significant changes, the estimate is also subject to change.

It may seem like a small thing, but many people take "quote" to mean it's a firm quote, no matter what happens. I know it sounds like semantics, but call it an "estimate".

Is the Client Briefing Not Clear? Ask Before You Start the Estimate

Sometimes you'll get a client briefing where you're not quite sure what they mean. For example, they may say they want "ground-breaking" or "culturally authentic" concepts.

What do they mean by that? You might be tempted to skip over it, assuming you understand what they mean. You may be concerned you'll look stupid by asking questions.

Ask. Have the discussion. Let the client elaborate on what they mean. Perhaps they can show you examples of what they mean. You'll look like you're interested in making sure you get everything right.

When you get into conceptual descriptions, meaning can be very different from one person to another. It's better to clarify these terms before the estimate and certainly before you start the project.

What If the Project Changes Partway Through?

It's not unusual for a larger project to change while you're in the middle of it. Often, this involves adding to the project.

Again, before agreeing to do the extra work, let the client know that you will be providing an estimate and will require approval before proceeding.

This is critical for three reasons:

1. First, the client is alerted that this new work will cost more, and you're not just "throwing it in." In some cases, the client may decide not to do the additional work because of the cost.
2. Second, you need to quickly figure out whether the extra work will affect the delivery date. Ideally, it won't, but depending on the nature of the work, it may. Can the date be moved if necessary? Remember to bring this up.
3. Last, even if they approve the costs, you want to ensure that your paperwork is up to date with the status of the

project. Don't fall into the trap of doing the work and then just adding it to the invoice without providing and getting approval on an estimate.

Otherwise, when it comes time to pay your invoice, there's a good chance that someone in their accounting department will flag it because your invoice doesn't align with your estimate. Make sure that all documentation is up to date so that your estimates match your invoice.

Some larger projects can change many times over their course. That might mean you have an initial estimate with five supplementary estimates to go along with it. That's fine. You want that track record for clarity and to support your final billing.

What if the client takes something away from the project? If you had the project broken down into phases and you're removing one of those phases, it should be easy to figure out how to adjust the estimate. If it's not that simple, you'll have to do some calculations to determine how to alter the estimate.

And again, write and get approval for the revised estimate.

Make Sure Your Estimates Have Enough Detail

Creating a detailed estimate for each project should be part of your process from the first day. The estimate is your summary of the project and can become a valuable reference document, especially for larger projects that sometimes go on for months.

Even if the client gives you a project brief and a budget that you agree to, you should take that brief and put it into your own words as your estimate back to them.

Your estimate serves as a guide for how you and your team will deliver the project, the steps along the way, delivery dates, and progress billing.

Equally valuable, the estimate also limits the project. I often had clients ask for something in the middle of the project that wasn't included in the estimate. Maybe they thought it was part of the project, or they're just trying to get a little extra, but a quick check reaffirmed the project scope.

That's why detail is essential; it clarifies what you meant by a deliverable.

If the client asks for a small change or addition, you may decide to include it without changing the estimate. Still, for anything more extensive, you need an addition to the original document.

Exactly How Much Detail Do You Need?

The amount of detail included in an estimate will vary depending on the scope of the project, and more particularly, the extent of the briefing document you received from the client.

For small, straightforward jobs, the estimate could be just one page. For larger projects, we often received briefs that ran for many pages. We found it an excellent practice to incorporate some of the language of those briefs into our estimate. This gave the client comfort that we had read the brief and considered all of the points in our estimate.

It's also vital that your estimate includes a schedule for the delivery of the various phases, and another schedule for payment. These should be reviewed and approved as part of the job.

Don't get into the habit of writing a short description and then a single dollar figure for the whole job. For example, don't write an estimate that looks like, "Create a new logo for ABC product: $10,000." This doesn't give the client any idea how you're going to do the project or how you came up with that number.

You want to include various steps such as research, the initial presentation of concepts, review meetings, finalizing one concept, allowing for two rounds of revisions, creating final art in appropriate formats, etc., with each line item having its own associated cost that adds up to the $10,000 total.

The details help the client understand how you got to your estimate, and all the work you'll be putting in to create your final deliverable.

Schedule a review of the estimate with the client, either in person or on the phone. Don't just send the estimate, and hope you get a positive response. You want confirmation that the client understands what's outlined. If necessary, talk through each point in your estimate and ask them if they have any questions.

What if the client says they want to see more concepts than you've proposed? Or they know approvals will go through many layers at the company, so it's best to allow for additional rounds of revisions? If that happens, you can alter the appropriate line items to include those milestones.

Once you have the estimate finalized with written approval and the deposit paid (if that's part of the estimate), you can begin.

Another reason to break down your estimate into deliverable phases is that you may have a payment schedule where you can bill and get paid once you've completed specific deliverables.

This is especially important on larger projects that stretch over months. You don't want to work on a $50,000 project and not get paid anything until completion. That's not good for your cash flow.

Any significant project that lasts more than a few weeks should include a payment schedule that allows you to progress bill as you complete specific milestones. It's only fair.

An Alternate View on Estimate Structure

Contrary to my experience in creating estimates, some consultants say that your estimate should contain plenty of detail but should not break out the numbers along the way. Instead, there should just be one number at the bottom of the estimate.

So, for example, they would write a three-page description of a project. On the last page, it would say $80,000. In their view, it's a more professional way to estimate. It feels more like you're acting as a consultant.

I disagree, and here's why. This method makes your estimate less transparent. Even with the appropriate amount of description, the client doesn't know how you came up with that number. Is it just a random figure? I think it invites too many questions that often force you to justify your rates.

Also, if the project changes course or gets canceled partway through, how much do they owe you? Where are you in terms of deliverables for which you should bill?

In general, I believe the more transparent you are, the easier it is for the client to say yes. They can follow along with how you broke down the project and what each step costs. They may have questions, but you should be able to answer them.

An Example of An Estimate Outline

Our estimate template included the following components:

On your digital letterhead, make a header called "Assignment Estimate" followed by this information:

Date: Date you're submitting the estimate

Client: Your client's company name

Project: The project name

Job #:Your job number from your project software

Prepared by: Your name

Prepared for:The person at the client who this is for

Project Overview

Start with a section that gives a brief overview of the project. It could be something like this:

Client X requires graphic design and production services to customize existing artwork and prepare new artwork for collateral for each of its eight partner organizations. This is to be based on the existing collateral style as provided.

Kick-Off Meeting

In your estimate, start with a section called Kick-Off Meeting. This should outline your proposed face-to-face or online project launch meeting.

In this section, describe what you want to cover in this meeting. Will you be bringing anything to this meeting? Should the client bring reference or background materials? Do they need specific people at the meeting, e.g., someone from tech?

It's essential to have a formal start to the project, and yes, you're billing for it. We often found these types of project launch meetings went on for a half day, and we might have three or four people at the table. So, you need to get paid for it.

Process and Deliverables

Then comes the main section. Here is where you describe the project as you understand it. Break it down into phases of deliverables. Each deliverable should have an estimate associated with it.

For example, for a design project, you may want to present initial layouts of three options that show what the final deliverable might be.

You can define these options in whatever way is appropriate. For example, if we were doing a website, we would mock-up three design options for a home page and two or three key inside pages. For an ad, we would show three versions of the ad.

You should get approval ahead of time on what you propose to show here. Some clients want to see more options or more pages per option, so your estimate should reflect the work required.

Concept Presentation

Then, there would be a phase where you have a working meeting to present your creative concepts.

If all goes well, the client chooses one option to be refined. Typically, you'll find that when you give three options, the client will lean toward one of them but want features from the others integrated. So, you want to include up to two rounds of revisions to come up with the final version.

Based on approval of that design option, the next section breaks down the rest of the project to final delivery. So, for a website, if they've approved key pages, your estimate should include the cost of production for the rest of the site.

It's critical to separate the project into logical deliverables, especially where key approvals are required to move onto the next phase.

. . .

Final Creative Client Presentation

Toward the end of the project, there should be a phase for a client presentation. Again, another working session, ideally face-to-face if possible. Here's where you show final designs and gather input before you go into production.

In your estimate for this phase, include up to two rounds of minor revisions. Why revisions, when what you're presenting is the final version of the piece?

You need the option for revisions here because it might not be until this phase that the project is shown to upper management. You wish they would get involved earlier, but often they don't. Once they see it, they may request some changes, so you may as well anticipate it.

Although we would typically say "up to two rounds of revisions," we have had clients ask us to include more, say five rounds, because they've been through this with management before and know that it could take up to five rounds of revisions.

You should know this ahead of time so you can build it into the estimate.

Schedule

Include a detailed schedule for the project with key delivery dates. The schedule should also take into consideration time for client approvals.

Be sure to review this with the client. Better to be realistic at the beginning than to constantly fight the schedule throughout the project.

. . .

Estimate Summary

Next, you'll want an estimate summary where you create one line for each deliverable with the dollar amount next to it.

After the estimate summary, include a few sentences that say something like this:

Please note: Additional revisions or significant changes in direction will be quoted in advance. Material costs, i.e., color composite copies, and expenses such as couriers and deliveries, will be billed as extra. Applicable taxes are extra.

Client Approval

Lastly, add a section that asks for specific client approval.

If there is a payment schedule for the project, you should include it on this page.

It should say something like this:

The proposed budget includes the steps and deliverables as outlined. Any further requirements for this project will be quoted separately. To initiate work, please indicate your approval by replying to this email or sign below. Thank you.

I confirm that the above-mentioned project will be delivered by Your Company (Your Company Address) as outlined in this proposal

Date:

Signature:

.   .   .

If you're using estimating software that allows a client to check a box to accept the estimate, you'll get a check mark rather than a signature. Either is fine.

Quick Note on Estimate Approvals

In our estimates, we always included a page for the client to sign. They could do this by printing the page, signing it, scanning it, and sending it back, or pasting in a digital signature. Or they could simply respond to the email, explicitly stating they've accepted our estimate.

Figure out what works for you, but make sure you have a clear record of approval to proceed with the estimate as submitted. Try not to accept just a phone call. If you only get a phone call, send an email acknowledging the call that you can save and keep with the estimate as confirmation of their approval.

If there is a payment schedule, and especially if a down payment is required, be sure to review this explicitly with the client. To get a down payment, you'll need to submit an invoice for their accounting department. In your discussion, after you've received overall approval, simply mention that an invoice for the deposit is following, and prompt processing can get the project underway.

Asked to Sign a Contract? Watch for These Clauses

Let's say you provided an estimate to a client, and it's approved. Some clients take your estimate and turn it into a contract that they want you to sign. Generally, they embed your estimate into a document and wrap other clauses around it.

Pay careful attention to these clauses. If you're not 100 percent sure what they mean, get a legal opinion.

In many cases, they are written to be heavily in favor of the client. In particular, you want to pay attention to clauses that address:

- Approval of work and how that affects payment. Some contracts may suggest that if the client is not happy with something, they reserve the right not to pay for anything. That's a definite "no".
- Responsibilities for indemnity that suggest you will indemnify your client for any related legal issues. That means, for example, if someone sues them because they think the logo you designed for the client looks too much like theirs, you'll pay the client's legal fees. As a small company, you can't afford to indemnify anyone, period.
- Look for any type of penalty clause. For example, can you be penalized if you miss a deadline? You don't want to agree to that. What if it was the client's fault?
- If you're working for a client through an agency, watch for clauses that say you can never work for that client directly. If there is such a clause, it should have a time limit, say one year after you last worked for the client through the agency.

Again, be very careful signing contracts that a client gives you. If you or your lawyer find objectionable clauses, insist that they're modified or taken out.

In my companies' case, this situation rarely came up. Mostly, our signed estimates acted as contracts. In the few instances where we did have to sign, we knew what we were signing, and it was never an issue.

Get Approvals Along the Way

As important as it is to get an approval of your estimate to start a project, once you get going, you'll need further approvals at specific stages of the project. Be clear with your clients where you need approvals before you go on to the next step. Don't be tempted to work ahead without approval of your previous work.

For example, in building a website, you'll want to make sure you have an approved layout and functionality before programming starts. You may think you'll save time doing these steps simultaneously, but if your site functionality changes, you could be redoing much of the programming.

Make sure your client knows that they're giving you the approval to move on. You don't want them coming back to you, claiming something wasn't approved, and asking for changes. Reworking what you've already done can lead to debates over whether they should pay for the "extra work" or whether it was your mistake to move on.

Whether my companies were designing logos, websites, or looking at photographic approaches, our typical estimate included three initial concepts for consideration.

I have read books where they say you should only present one option with plenty of rationale to show how you got there. Maybe you could sell that, but it never worked for me. If your estimate includes just one proposed creative solution, it seems like it's "take it or leave it." Some clients will feel like they're being bullied into only one idea and have no say in it.

Other times in a misguided effort to reduce an estimate, a client will say, "We don't need three options, just show us one idea, and we'll be fine with it." Reluctantly, you go along with it.

After presenting it to them, even if they loved it, inevitably, they will ask, "Did you have any other ideas?" Well, of course, we did, but you only wanted to see one.

For me, three has been a magic number. Not one, two, four, or five. The number is three. Settling on two options feels like "choose this or that." It forces a choice that many people don't want to make. Two never feels like it's enough.

Three immediately feels like you've given them lots to look at and consider. Clients often bounce back and forth as they look at them. It opens up a broader conversation and more comparisons between the elements shown. Clients are more involved and feel that you've thoroughly explored the possibilities for the project.

We try not to commit to showing more than three. It can get confusing, and clients become overwhelmed by choice. I used to joke that the way we count is one, two, three, and a bunch more...

Having said that, if a client insists on seeing more options, and they'll pay you for more, go ahead. I've done it, mainly in the early phases of naming and logos, but make sure you leave more time for the client to narrow down the choices.

Typically, my companies would try to have the first group of ideas presented "roughly" (they looked finished, but there was still room for tweaking) and then cut the options down, which we showed in a more finished state.

In some cases, clients attempt to create strange mash-ups. "Could you show us a version where you combine concepts 2, 4, and 7?" Be careful you don't let clients turn your sleek horses into awkward, lumpy camels.

No Straw Dogs—You Should Love Them All

When you commit to creating options for consideration, you must be prepared for the client to choose any one of them. That means that each of them should be well thought out and an excellent choice for the assignment.

If you're going into the meeting with one option you like and others that you know aren't strong, inevitably one of two things will happen: either the client will choose one of the weaker ones, or even worse, they will immediately recognize that there's only one strong contender, and you'll have to defend why you're showing half-baked ideas.

You have to be able to deliver what you promised: compelling ideas, every time. Make sure you have a solid rationale for every concept you present.

How to Deal with Critical Timelines

There are projects where timelines are cast in stone. For example, a new product launch may be scheduled for a specific day, and many suppliers are contributing to the unveiling. Your project is to build the website and have it tested and ready for that day.

Let's assume that when you were briefed for the project, the client approved your estimate and timelines. On that day, the timelines seemed reasonable.

You had broken down the project by deliverables and allowed appropriate time for each phase. You and the client reviewed the schedule you created, and all of you agreed on the personal responsibilities to meet those dates.

On the client side, their tasks were to get you the materials you need by specific dates and to make timely approvals along the way.

Then, early in the project, the client begins to miss their deadlines. They're not giving you feedback by the agreed-upon dates, which means you can't move forward. Now what?

It's critical at this point that you or your project manager speak with the client as soon as they miss their first date to get them back on track. Don't let time go by as if everything is all right.

Remember, the deadline is fixed and can't be moved. In a polite but firm way, you have to bring this up with the client.

If you don't, here's what will happen: the client will assume that somehow, by magic or by you working 24/7, you will get it done by the deadline.

The worst-case scenario is that you don't make the deadline, the product launch is missing the website, and somehow it was all your fault. Now your relationship is on the rocks, and they may not want to pay you or give you any further projects.

Do not allow anyone to put you in that position. Whenever you're doing a project with an unmovable deadline, you need to stay on top of that schedule every day right from the beginning.

What if, partway through the project, the client wants to add more deliverables? You have to determine whether you can add them and still make the deadline. If you can't, the client needs to understand that adding anything to the project while it's underway could have a negative impact on the delivery.

Here is where your diplomacy may be tested. Keep in mind that you and the client are on the same side and are not adversaries. You both want a terrific project delivered by the deadline. Your client is not purposely trying to derail the project by adding to it.

Perhaps whatever they're trying to include is something they forgot earlier, and now they desperately need it. They're hoping you can save them. If you can accommodate them (remember to provide an estimate and get approval for the extra work), you'll be a hero.

In any case, you and the client need to work together to figure out a solution, understanding that you can't move the deadline.

What About Timelines That Aren't So Critical?

Every project should have a schedule and a deadline. Once you start a job, you want to work on it efficiently and complete it in a reasonable time.

But what if the client slows it down? They don't seem to be in any hurry to get the job done. It's not in your best interest to have a one-month project drag out for six months. It's an inefficient way to work.

This is where you need to bill by deliverables. You should at least get paid along the way for work done to date. Sometimes, just bringing up billing with the client will wake them up and get them back on schedule.

The other problem with projects that start to drag is an increased likelihood that the job won't get completed. Clients lose interest, their focus turns to new initiatives, and soon the project that once seemed vital is completely forgotten. That's not good for you or your relationship with the client.

It is always in your best interest to create a schedule with a deadline and ensure everyone sticks to it.

Thorough Estimates = Fewer Money Debates

Certainly, my companies would have "money talks" with clients before projects started. Good clients would tell us they have $X for a project along with a written brief. We'd review it and proceed to create an estimate. If there were differences, we would talk about them to agree on the scope and budget.

Other clients would give us a brief and ask us to come up with an estimate. It wasn't a question of doing or not doing the project. They had an adequate budget and wanted the project done. They simply wanted to see how we'd break out the various deliverables and charge for them.

There would sometimes be some back and forth on the project scope and the estimate, but we would soon settle on it and get approval to proceed.

The result was that over the years, we had very few debates about money after the fact. It just didn't come up. Our communications about money had been very clear from beginning to end, so there were no arguments. That made sure we got paid and generally in a timely fashion.

I've had discussions with other creative agencies who have had endless disputes about getting paid, have had to write off significant amounts, and sometimes got tangled up in lawsuits. That rarely happened to us.

Don't let it happen to you. It's tiring, and it leads to unhappy clients and sleepless nights for you.

If you find you have a client who still wants to argue about money after the job is done, even though you've been very clear in your estimates along the way and delivered according to the brief, then you need to have a very specific discussion about that.

You want the client to be happy. You want to be happy too. What can you do to ensure there is better clarity about the money?

If, after that, the behavior continues, you may want to consider whether you wish to carry on with that client.

Should Equipment Rentals Go Into Estimates?

I know that for photographers and filmmakers, equipment rentals are sometimes necessary for the project.

I think you should be careful with this on an estimate. If you're renting something small, say a few extra lights, I'd bury it in the estimate and not mention it. Just increase your overall estimate by the amount the rental will cost you. You don't want to make it a sticking point.

The client may think that you should own this equipment and shouldn't get charged extra for it. After all, you own your cameras, phones, laptops, and software and don't break out costs for them.

On the other hand, if it's something major, put it in and add a 15 to 25 percent markup on it. Renting a helicopter? A big crane? Everyone expects there will be a cost, and no one would assume you own it. The work you'll put into sourcing the rental justifies your markup.

In general, you want to make estimates easy to approve with no unexpected line items.

When to Use Markups

Whenever you take responsibility for someone else's work and bill that work through your company, you should mark it up.

So, if you hire a recording studio to do a voice-over or music, you should mark up their invoice to you as part of your invoice to the client. If you're handling the printing, you should mark up the printer's invoice.

Your markup should be between 15 and 25 percent. You charge a markup because you are assuming the risk for their work.

If, for example, something goes wrong on a printing job, you will work it out with the printer on how to fix that. If it was your fault, you might have to pay. If it was the printer's fault, they have to make good. But in any case, you resolve it without involving the client.

If a client ever asks whether you mark up suppliers' invoices, just answer truthfully and explain it's to ensure their work meets expectations.

Pay Attention to Purchase Orders

Most large clients, or smaller ones that are very organized, use purchase orders. A purchase order is simply a document from the client's accounting department that formalizes that they have hired you for a project. It outlines the details, including costs and deadlines.

The critical thing to know is that you'll need information from the purchase order—at the very least, the purchase order number—to include on your invoice to smooth the payment process. Accounting departments rely on lining up purchase orders with invoices to keep track of projects.

We would sometimes scan their purchase order and add it to our invoice to make it easier for their accounting department to reference.

This is also why it's essential to provide additional estimates and get revised or further purchase orders if a job changes. At the end of the project, you want your estimates to align with the purchase orders or risk problems getting it through accounting.

Estimate by Deliverable, Not by the Hour

We estimated virtually all of our projects by the deliverable. It meant that there was a clean beginning and end to the project. Our challenge was to create a detailed description of the project so that the client was clear on the steps and details of the job.

Our estimates never showed the number of hours for a task or an hourly rate. It was irrelevant. In our view, once we had defined the series of tasks that made up the project, we gave a fixed price. We were happy with that, and so were the clients.

This way of estimating allowed the client to budget with certainty. From experience, we knew that it was the way clients looked at their budgets internally.

They might start the year knowing that they have $250,000 in their funding, and they have three major projects and five smaller ones. They would allocate budgets to each project, leaving some as a slush fund in case other projects came up.

Or they might answer to an internal client who controls the budget. That client would come to our direct client and say I've got a budget of $25,000 to do project X, and then we would collectively work out the deliverables knowing the budget number ahead of time.

Sometimes clients ask how much you charge by the hour. If you're a solo operator, you could answer that, but try not to. Why not?

Well, essentially, it's a meaningless number. The obvious missing element is how many hours it takes you. You could charge $100 an hour, do the job in 10 hours, or $150 an hour and do the job in five hours. In the end, what matters is the final cost for the deliverables.

Also, billing by the hour penalizes you for being efficient. That would mean if you're very fast, you get paid less. Why would you do that? And why would a client agree to pay you more if you're slow?

I think you should bill by carefully defined deliverables that make up a project.

Also, avoid agreeing to take on a project where the client suggests that "You keep track of your hours and then bill us," especially if it's left open-ended. That gets you back to billing by the hour, which you don't want to do.

These days, only law firms seem to get away with that kind of hourly billing, and most clients hate them for it. ("I thought this assignment would be five hours, not 20...)

If you casually start a job on an hourly basis and just let the client know when you're done, I can guarantee you'll have problems when it comes to billing and collecting.

If a client suggests paying you that way, create an estimate showing phases by deliverable, with dollar amounts per phase totaling to a final number. Get approval in writing before starting.

At all times, you should be in control of how you do your estimating and billing. Don't let a client change your processes.

How Do You Calculate Your Billing Rates?

Billing rates can be very tricky, especially when you're starting your business. Even if you're billing based on deliverables, the question remains, how do you calculate how much you should bill?

Here you could use the services of your accountant or business advisor.

Let's go back to basics for a minute. Your overall goal for the company is to be profitable. After everyone, including you, has been paid their salary and any applicable bonuses or dividends, after all of the overhead, expenses, and taxes, your company should be left with a net profit.

Some of that profit will remain in the bank, and some of it you can take out as dividends or profit sharing.

Getting this right comes with experience and will likely improve over time. When companies start, they often guesstimate.

It's okay to start this way, but not a long-term solution for running a business. Inevitably, you end up working longer hours than you had assumed. You'll begin to wonder why you're working so hard but have so little to show for it.

In general, there are two ways that creative agencies calculate rates.

The first is to determine an hourly rate for everyone working on a project—one for a junior, another for a senior, etc.

The fast and easy way to figure out an individual's billing rate is to multiply their salary by three and divide by 100. So, a $50,000 salary means $150 per hour.

When you're just starting and have so many things to figure out, use that as a beginning point and then tweak it as you see fit. As your business evolves, you'll adjust your rates anyway.

The second way to look at billing rates is to develop a blended rate for the company. You still have to figure out how many hours per task, and then multiply that by the blended rate.

Typically, companies start with the first version—a different rate for everyone working on the project based on their salaries. As they get more mature, they transition to the second version, the blended rate.

There are a few reasons for this. First, it's easier for the company to come up with estimates. But more importantly, large clients, both private sector and government, often ask for the blended rate on their RFPs. They're expecting a "shop rate."

In creating a blended rate, you're aiming for one number for your company to apply to most of your projects.

To calculate the rate, you'll need to apply formulas that include your salary, your employee salaries, the number of billable hours anyone has in a week, a ratio that relates to your overhead, and your desired profit margin.

I'm not going to get into all of the variations of the required math here.

The best explanations and formulas that I've found are on the AIGA website at AIGA.org. (AIGA was once known as the American Institute of Graphic Arts. It is now known simply as "AIGA, the professional association for design.") On the site, search for "pricing models" and you'll find several in-depth articles on coming up with billing rates.

Pick a formula that applies to your business and run your numbers. Review them with your accountant or financial advisor. Then try them out on a real estimate. Do the numbers make sense when you apply them to a project?

Your goal is to come up with a number you can use across most projects you do.

When Not to Use Your Billing Rate

Your billing rate is based on the assumption that most projects involve people from various levels of your company, from the most senior to junior.

But some projects aren't like that. Sometimes you need to deliver very low-level simple production work, the equivalent of making photocopies. For those types of jobs, adjust your estimate accordingly. You don't need to say anything to the client; you just need to develop a reasonable estimate for that type of work.

What if Your Internal Billing Rate is Too High for Your Market?

Whichever method you use to calculate your rate, these are the only variables that go into it:

1. The billing rate of your employees, which includes overhead
2. Your desired profit margin

To lower your rate, your first option is to hire employees that will cost you less. However, before you look for the lowest-cost employees, ask yourself whether these people can do the jobs required in an efficient manner that meets your standards.

If your company is made up only of very senior (read: very expensive) employees, you will have a high billing rate. If you can justify it and get paid for it (because likely you're a company of specialists in an on-demand field), you're all set. But if not, something has to change.

A second option is to look for ways to reduce your overhead. This can be your most significant cost factor. Look at rent, monthly leases, etc., to see whether there's something you can trim to cut costs.

Do not be tempted to reduce your profit margin. If you do, you'll soon be out of business. Companies need profit to survive.

And finally, what you're billing your clients is made up of your billing rate times the number of hours you've estimated, in other words, your efficiency.

Review your projects to see how you delivered them—did your estimates reflect the reality of how the jobs were done? Are you and your employees working efficiently?

This is where you have to look at time sheets and do the math to determine how efficiently your company operates. There's a section on time sheets and billing efficiency later in the book.

Maybe You Have the Wrong Clients

After you've looked at your operations and how they relate to rates, the most obvious place to look is your clients.

Are you working with the right clients? If you believe your rates are fair and want to maintain them, you may have to reconsider your client mix. In general, more sophisticated, bigger clients pay more.

No matter what you charge, you'll be too expensive for some clients. If people ask why you can't do $50 logos or $500 videos, simply tell them that you'd be losing money on jobs at those rates. You can't do that.

You have to say no to clients that aren't right for you.

Can You Make Retainers Work for You?

In my companies, we didn't use retainers. However, they may be ideal for you, for some or all of your clients. In its basic form, a retainer outlines a set amount the client pays you per hour for a predetermined number of hours.

Retainers can work very well for both parties. The client is assured of your availability to perform the tasks. Their fees to you are predictable. You, as the agency, are assured of dependable revenue.

Retainers can be implemented for all types of work. Most typically, they're used for ongoing process-driven tasks such as maintaining social media accounts, updating websites, or monitoring media.

Retainers simplify the entire estimating and billing processes. Based on initial discussions and agency recommendations, the client chooses the number of hours they would like per month.

These hours are all calculated at a blended rate and billed at the beginning of every month. Many agencies will insist on getting paid on that date, either by direct deposit or by client credit card.

Typically, the agency would send progress reports weekly or twice a month, outlining work completed and hours used.

Although the client initially chooses the number of hours per month, this can be adjusted up or down once the amount of work becomes apparent.

Typical Client Questions About Retainer Arrangements

When you first meet with a client to discuss a retainer contract, you may as well answer these questions before they ask. Clients will want to know:

- What happens to their monthly hours if they're not all used? Generally, you would roll them over into the next month.
- What happens if they use more than their monthly hours? You will bill them for the extra hours at the agreed-upon rate.
- Can they put the retainer on pause? Some clients have very seasonal businesses, with little activity in other months. Ideally, you let them pause their account with appropriate notice to make adjustments.
- Are hours refundable? That's your call, but usually, they're not.
- What services do you include in the retainer? Generally, you'll want to include all of your services. It may be

worth spelling them out in a document so that client is aware of what you offer.

Big Benefits of Retainer Contracts

The first significant benefit is that you no longer write an estimate for each project. That's a huge timesaver. This frees you up for other tasks and helps your agency work much more efficiently.

On the client side, they no longer need to approve individual estimates. Big time saver for them too. You'll still have discussions about the scope of the project and the estimated hours it will take to complete it, but that's much easier than getting approval for each estimate.

Speaking of scope, no more scope creep. (Imagine that!) Whatever needs to be done will simply be part of the retainer hours. It might still be frustrating doing five rounds of revisions or getting changes of direction, but it's much less contentious, and you know you're getting paid.

When a project is completed, you're not writing individual invoices either. For the retainer, you create a monthly invoice with regular progress reports along the way.

Your billing and your cash flow become much more predictable.

Retainers Require a High Degree of Trust

The retainer arrangement works well when there is mutual trust. The client must be comfortable that you are taking the appropriate amount of time for any given project and not merely churning hours. They give up some control over costs, compared to receiving estimates by the project, where they could push back on specific line items.

Many agencies have found that it takes time working with a client to reach the required level of trust before switching over to a retainer arrangement.

In other cases, agencies simply state that this is how we work, and a prospective client can speak to some of their existing clients for a testament to the benefits of the arrangement.

You'll have to decide how much you want to push clients towards any method of estimating and billing. Some agencies are happy to have different arrangements with various clients, while others are strict in how they want to conduct business.

Is Value Pricing the Holy Grail for Pricing Models?

These days, many pricing consultants recommend that service suppliers use a value pricing model when estimating and billing clients.

Value pricing is based on the value of the project to the client. It assumes that you and the client agree that the project you're doing for them could be worth $X to them and then agree that your fee will be a percentage, say 10 percent to 25 percent, of the project's added value.

This model is based on many assumptions:

- The client can accurately estimate the tangible value that your project will deliver.
- The client is willing to have a discussion with you about this value.
- Your completed project will meet both parties' definition of success.
- Your fee will be higher than if you'd calculated it another way (otherwise, why would you do it).

- Your expertise deserves the premium inherent in value pricing.

From my perspective, estimating on a project basis, as we did, has a notion of value pricing built into it. When we estimated by project, we didn't disclose an hourly rate or the number of hours it would take us. We simply said, to deliver this project is $X. There wasn't a notion of what it was worth to a client.

I've read about pure value pricing, watched videos of people explaining it, but I have never had those discussions with clients.

For most of the projects we did, it simply didn't apply. These were large corporations, organizations, or governments with requirements to communicate with their audiences, which they did through various media.

As I see it, here are the challenges with this pricing model if you want to implement it:

- In many cases, it's difficult to predetermine the value of a project with any degree of accuracy. And since the client holds all the cards as to the project's importance, how would you agree or disagree with any client number?
- For many projects, there is no real financial value. The company may simply be obligated to communicate a program. Would you not take on that project?
- If the client could determine the value, why would they share it with you? They're looking for the best price for the task at hand, not necessarily to share any resulting profits with you.
- Is there any guarantee that your project will deliver the expected value? What if it doesn't? Will you offer a rebate? (No, right?)
- Sometimes a small project could deliver enormous value. For example, a simple e-commerce website built

on WordPress, Shopify, or any other modern platform could bring in millions of dollars if it's selling an in-demand product. Why would a client agree to share those profits, when realistically, that site could be built in two weeks by any competent developer?

- If you believe in the value of your deliverable, why not propose to do the project on a commission basis? You pay to create the deliverable and then get $X for every sale or sign-up, as the case may be.

If you're interested in value pricing, do a quick search. There's plenty of information out there. If you can make it work, I salute you.

For me, it was always more straightforward to define a project and provide an estimate for its completion.

Chapter Takeaways

- There is an art to writing good estimates. Learn it, refine it, and stick to it. It's worth spending time here to get it right for your agency. Thorough estimates pay off.
- After a while, you'll have standard sections for your estimates describing the various parts of projects. Your estimating will get faster and more accurate.
- There are a few ways to set rates. How you do it will likely evolve. You need to be sure your company stays profitable and you're working reasonable hours.
- Spend time with your accountant or financial advisor to review your billings to ensure you're hitting your profitability targets.
- Some clients aren't right for you. Learn to say no.

18

BILLING AND PAYMENT TERMS

"Don't think for a moment that you've gotta be perfect to be paid."

— Clifford Cohen

If All Your Clients Are on Retainers, You Can Ignore This Section

This section covers:

- Getting deposits to start projects
- Billing by deliverable
- Payment terms
- Prompt collection of invoices
- Cash flow
- Volume discounts
- Collection calls

None of this is applicable if you have clients paying you a set amount on a retainer at the beginning of every month. You won't be concerned about deposits, interim billing, or payment terms.

Collections won't be an issue because you'll get paid at the beginning of the month. And no volume discounts—it's all calculated in the agreed-upon hourly rate.

It might be just the incentive you need to try to have all of your clients on retainers.

But, for most creative agencies who estimate and bill by the project, this chapter is very relevant and could help you keep your business running smoothly.

For New Clients, Get a Deposit Before You Start the Job

When you first work with a new client, you should get a deposit before starting the project.

Ideally, you will have brought this up in preliminary discussions, in the back and forth of how you do business, what they expect, and what you deliver. That way, when it comes up on the first estimate, it's no surprise.

This is where your confidence in talking about money comes into play. I've heard creators say they don't feel comfortable asking for money when they haven't done the work yet. You have to get over that. It's just business.

Getting deposits is relatively conventional in many business transactions such as hiring a lawyer, buying a house, ordering a car, or home renovations. It's simply the way business is done, and you should adopt it.

You should ask for a deposit that is meaningful to the project, at least between 25 and 50 percent of the estimate, and perhaps as much as 100 percent.

For example, on a $10,000 project, you could ask for a deposit of between $2,500 and $5,000 before starting. On a $50,000 project, a $12,500 deposit is reasonable. You'll need to present an invoice for that deposit to keep the paperwork current.

Why do you want a deposit? Well, why not? Better the money in your bank account than theirs. Simply, it's a show of faith on their part. You can also explain to a prospective client that the deposit reserves your time to dedicate to the project.

From your point of view, it helps with your cash flow. Also, since it's your first work for the new client, you want to make sure you get paid, so having at least a deposit is a good start.

Good clients will accept those terms and pay the deposit quickly. Some will push back. They may say, "We don't pay deposits." "The work has to be done before we can pay," or "Our accounting system won't allow it."

If this becomes a big issue, you'll have to decide whether or not to work with them. Is this an indication of how you're going to get paid, or is there a legitimate reason for the client not giving you a deposit?

If your "red flag radar" is going off, and your gut feeling tells you this will not be a good client, you're probably best telling the prospect that you absolutely need the deposit before starting and walk away. If they want to work with you, they'll come back to you, deposit in hand.

You might consider a fallback position of starting without a deposit and then billing and collecting after the first phase of the project, but you shouldn't move forward to further stages. This has to be a hard stop until they pay you.

Having said this, in my experience, some clients don't pay deposits, and you just have to work another way.

For example, government clients and large public corporations like utilities or health services often don't pay deposits. However, they do pay progress bills. Also, you have the reassurance that they are a big reputable organization supported by plenty of paperwork to ensure you get paid.

I would ask for a deposit for the first project with most clients. If you establish this as a precedent, you can continue this way with them on further projects.

Think like a lawyer. Every project starts with a deposit. It helps your cash flow.

Billing by Deliverable

With your estimates broken down into deliverables, you should also bill that way. However, here is where you'll have to use some common sense.

You may have a $10,000 project broken down into five deliverables. You don't want to create an invoice after each deliverable. It's too much paperwork for you and the client.

So, you may have a $2,500 deposit, which covers your first deliverable, then bill another $5,000 after the second and third deliverables, and then the last $2,500 when the job is complete. For smaller projects, you might have a deposit invoice and a final one.

Where billing by deliverable makes a significant difference is on larger assignments. Let's say you have a $50,000 project that takes months to deliver. You should get paid along the way after key deliverables rather than wait for everything at the end.

Most clients, even the biggest corporate clients, understand that and know that companies like yours need to keep their cash flow going.

Payment Terms and the Importance of Getting Paid on Time

You're in business to get paid. But critically, you need to get paid in a timely and relatively predictable fashion.

In addition to deposits and payments by deliverable, you also need to include terms of payment—namely, how soon you expect to get paid.

You must discuss and negotiate these terms when you first start working with a client. Be sure you have an explicit discussion—don't leave it for discovery on your first invoice.

For a deposit, you want payment terms to be due upon invoice.

After the deposit, typical terms of payment are:

- Net 10 days
- Net 30 days
- Net 30 days, 2 percent discount 10 days

"Net 10 days" or "Net 30 days" means you expect to get paid the full amount within 10 or 30 days of the client receiving the invoice.

"Net 30 days, 2 percent discount 10 days" means you expect to get paid within 30 days and are offering a 2 percent discount if the client pays within 10 days.

For some clients, offering a discount will be very appealing as it's a way for them to keep their costs down. However, not all clients can manage that—they know they either can't pay that quickly because of their internal approval systems, or they would rather not pay within 10 days.

These terms are all negotiable, and they're not necessarily the same for all clients. Some clients may tell you what terms they want. You may go back and forth a bit, but you need to come to an agreement.

I've had clients say, "We pay net 45 days or net 60 days." If you hear that, it should give you pause. You need to ask them why, when 30 days is much more typical.

It raises a red flag, and you have to ask yourself whether you want to work with clients like this. They are essentially using you as the bank, which isn't fair. It's as if you're giving them an interest-free loan for a few months.

However, if you decide to work with them, simply charge them a bit more than you would bill others. A banking fee, so to speak. You don't need to talk about it, just do it.

The reality is that even if it says Net 30 days, often you don't get paid for 45 or 60 days. So, if it already says Net 60 days, well, when are you going to get paid?

Cash Flow is King—Another Reason You Need to Get Paid on Time

You've likely heard the phrase, "Cash is king." I agree, but more importantly, to small businesses, cash *flow* is king. Money is always going out, so it has to keep coming in to get that flow going. (There's a song in there somewhere.)

Besides wanting to get paid so you can pay yourself, your staff, and overhead, you have other financial obligations. Let's talk about taxes again.

If you charge your clients a state or provincial tax, you have to submit that to the government. That money is due to the government in the billing cycle when it was billed to the client.

If you're paying those taxes monthly, you owe the government the taxes for everything billed that month. You get time after the month's end to pay, but there's a definite due date that you can't miss.

So, if a client doesn't pay you for three months, you will probably have paid taxes on money you haven't collected. You could be out hundreds of dollars that you've paid in taxes on behalf of your client, but they haven't paid you.

Remember, you pay the taxes based on the dates the invoices went out, not when you collected. You really can't afford to be in that situation.

Now let's look at suppliers that you've engaged on behalf of clients. Let's say you're paying someone for audio recording or video production.

Ideally, you want to pay your suppliers quickly, especially the ones you count on over and over again. Why? Not only is it good business practice, but suppliers notice. They see who pays quickly and who drags it out.

Also, some suppliers might offer you a discount for quick payment. You may want to take advantage of that.

There will come a time when you need a favor from a supplier. You're going to ask them to work all night or over the weekend to get a last-minute job done for a client. You want them to bust their butts for you. Do you think they'll do that for someone who takes ages to pay them? No.

Prompt payment goes a long way to creating happy relationships with your suppliers. Being able to pay your suppliers quickly is another reason you need to get paid according to the terms you agreed upon with your clients.

Cash Flow Problems, or Is It Something Else?

Something to think about: your overhead expenses are mostly fixed, or at the very least predictable, but the timing of your receivables is less so. If you're strict on collecting your receivables, your cash flow should be relatively smooth.

Occasionally, you'll run into periods where the receivables you were expecting just aren't coming in. Despite your efforts to collect, things are tight.

If this happens once in a while, you have a cash flow issue that should straighten itself out soon. This is why you need to have a cushion of reserve cash in the bank.

But if you find this happening frequently, you're just fooling yourself if you call it a cash flow problem and assume it will fix itself. There is something fundamentally wrong that needs to be changed.

The likely culprits:

- You're not busy enough. You need more clients, or for your existing clients to give you more work. To see it another way, you have too many staff for your business.
- You aren't doing a good job collecting your receivables—how much is out there over 30 days?
- You're underestimating your jobs—everyone seems busy, but there's not enough money coming in.
- Your fixed overhead costs such as rent or leases are too high for your business.
- You're paying yourself too much.

If you're struggling for more than a month with cash flow, it's not a cash flow problem. It's something else. You need to sit with your accountant or advisor to review the numbers and find a solution. This will not fix itself, and you have to make some decisions.

The Boy Scout Story About Payment Terms

One of the agencies I worked for was run by a highly ethical man who was a Boy Scout when he was younger, and it showed. His word was his bond, his handshake as good as a contract.

When the agency was invited to pitch a new client, often worth millions of dollars a year, he would, at some point, talk about payment terms. Most agencies don't bring that up in a pitch meeting when they're hoping to win new business. But he did.

He let them know that if they decided to work together, his agency would knock themselves out for the client, be utterly honorable in their dealings, and get the best terms from suppliers they dealt with on their behalf. In return, he expected to get paid, net 10 days, no exceptions.

At that point, most of the agency team was wishing a hole would open up under their chairs so they could disappear. They quietly cringed.

But here's the interesting part. It generally went down well. Clients simply understood the man's integrity, and his agency often won the business and then got paid promptly. They did not have cash flow problems.

I'm not saying you should do that in a pitch meeting, but he could pull it off, and it worked.

When Clients Abuse the Agreed-Upon Payment Terms

If 30 days stretches for a few days, but you get paid, well, that's just business. But if it goes to 45 or 60, you need to call the client and ask whether there's a problem. You have to be polite but strict. Don't let it go.

You may be surprised at what you hear when you call. "I don't have your invoice. Can you resend it?" or "There's a problem with your invoice" or "There must be a problem in accounting. I thought you already got paid."

In other words, if you don't call, you may not get paid for a very long time, if ever.

What if a client agrees to 2 percent discount, 10 days, but takes the 2 percent and pays you in 30 or 45 days? You have to call them and discuss. It's unacceptable. Don't ignore it.

These days, when invoices are submitted and processed electronically, and you're generally getting paid by direct transfer, there's no excuse for late payments.

Business has to be a two-way street: you deliver excellent work on time, and your client should pay you according to the agreed-upon terms.

Should You Offer Volume Discounts?

Some clients may ask you about volume discounts, which would apply to invoices once they hit a predetermined threshold.

Typically, the notion of volume discounts comes up in RFPs. It seems to have become a standard line item. Generally, they ask whether you offer them, and if so, what terms you would be prepared to abide by if you start working together.

My simple answer is, yes, you should give volume discounts, provided you set the criteria. To me, a volume discount is a reward for a substantial amount of work over a defined period, such as a year, tied to prompt payments of invoices.

You'll want to structure your volume discount offer to include both the volume and the prompt payment: For example, at the start of the year, before reaching the agreed-upon threshold, your terms could be:

- Net 30 days, 2 percent discount 10 days

After they've hit the threshold, let's say $100,000, you can change the terms to reflect the volume discount:

- Net 30 days, 5 percent discount 10 days

You always want to tie any volume discount to prompt payment. You do not want to be in a situation where you're giving a discount, but you're not getting paid for 90 days.

You will have to keep track of the billing throughout the year to ensure you switch to the volume discount terms once they pass the threshold. When the year is up, the meter starts again at zero.

Like all other terms, these are negotiable. Be prepared for a bit of back and forth in agreeing to this type of arrangement.

Want to Avoid Tough Collection Conversations with Clients?

Let someone else do it. This may sound like a copout, but it's a good collections strategy. However, it only works if you have someone else working with you, even on a part-time basis.

You are the creative person. You come up with the innovative solutions, the writing, designing, photography, or whatever you supply to your clients. You get emotionally involved with them and the work you do together. You're business friends.

So, it becomes tough for some creators to call a client and remind them that payment is overdue, when rightfully, you shouldn't have to do it.

The client should have paid you as they originally agreed, but now they seem to be going back on their word. Sometimes it's hard to confront them. You sound like you're either begging or threatening.

That's where your executive assistant, bookkeeper, or financial manager comes in. Make it their job to call and collect the outstanding payments. For them, it's not personal, they're just managing the money, and collections are part of it.

You may hear from your client after the call. They'll likely be a bit sheepish, "Hey, I got a call from your bookkeeper, and we'll take care of that right away. Sorry about that."

Doing it this way lets you keep your purely creative relationship with your client. It also saves you time. Making calls like this can suck up hours. This collection strategy worked very well for us. We always had our bookkeeper call clients to collect overdue invoices.

Chapter Takeaways

- Getting paid in a timely fashion is critical. Make sure your clients understand your payment terms in advance, that they agree to them, and pay on time.
- Don't let your receivables build up. You need to keep your cash flowing. However, if you're experiencing ongoing cash shortages, you have a different problem. Don't ignore it. Fix it, the sooner the better.
- Use volume discounts as an incentive for clients to give you more business. Set the threshold so it's realistic for them to achieve it, but high enough to make it a stretch.
- Get someone else to make the collections calls. You're the creative person.

19

ADDING PEOPLE

"It's expensive to hire the wrong people. If they leave it's expensive. If they stay it's expensive."

— Nathan Mellor

Adding People to Your Business

Let's say you've decided to expand your company beyond just yourself. That might be because you're so busy that you need help doing what you do day-to-day. In this case, you would want to hire another version of yourself.

Or, you might be much more productive if you had help with the paperwork, such as writing estimates, proposals, and invoices. That would mean finding someone with a business admin background.

Perhaps, you're regularly asked to do projects where you need a complementary skill set to take on the work. Maybe you're a writer, and for many of your projects, there's a design requirement too. If you had a designer available, you could also get that part of the assignment.

You'll likely get a feel for this when working with your clients.

For example, are they pairing you with other freelancers to get the projects done? That was my experience when I worked freelance as a copywriter. Clients would give me the designer's name on the project and ask me to coordinate with them.

It didn't take too long to figure out that if I had a company with my own designer, we would get the whole project.

Even by adding just one person, you will automatically become qualified for more work. Many clients are only interested in working with someone who can deliver the whole project. They don't want to play matchmaker. They want to hand off the project to a team that can do it all. That's why they haven't called you in the past.

When our agencies grew, we generally had more graphic designers than any other type of employee. As a rule of thumb, one good writer can keep two or three designers busy.

Then beyond that, you'll want one or more highly organized project managers to maintain control of the three-ring circus you're building (Joke—of course, I meant your highly efficient, profitable creative agency).

When Do You Bring on More People?

The simple answer is you bring on people when the work demands it. But often, it's tricky to know whether it's ongoing work or just temporary. It also depends on how you work—do you have a full-time staff, or do you pull together freelancers as you need them? Do you have an office, or do people work from home?

In my companies, we added to the staff, mainly graphic designers, when we worked extra hours on an ongoing basis and could see this continuing for months.

We didn't tend to work with freelancers for our core deliverables, although we would hire programmers, photographers, and illustrators by the project.

Other companies have organized themselves to manage a stable of freelance talent that they can call upon as needed.

This is not trivial—if you're going to work this way, you have to create a network you can depend on and manage their time and deliverables since they're not likely working in the same office as you.

For many creators, I think the ideal situation is a combination of a small, dedicated staff along with freelancers and specialists you can count on as needed.

It's only been over the past decade or so that we've had tools such as Slack, Trello, and Zoom to make this much more manageable.

Also, it's become a preference for how many people want to work. Today there are far more freelancers than previously in all disciplines.

By having a dedicated core at the center, you're operating a lean company, saving on rent, equipment, and benefits. Learn how to manage that, and you can expand and contract as work demands.

Hiring on a Contract Basis

Before you make the leap to hire someone full-time, ask yourself whether you could get someone on a contract or freelance basis.

There are many ways you can define a contract. It might be for a specific project. That may mean you want that person every day, all day, for a month until the project is over. Or, for a business or finance person, it may be one day a week to get caught up on paperwork.

Consider for a minute how they make movies in Hollywood. Nothing exists until the project is ready to go with financing in place. Then, teams are pulled together to work on the project.

Once the movie is finished, the teams disband. There are no full-time employees. They are brought together for the task of making the movie.

So, if you find yourself landing a big job where you need help, think about it like filmmaking. Consider whether it makes sense to hire for the project. You may fall into an ongoing relationship with that person, where you call them a few times a year as needed.

By the way, this is an excellent way to try someone out without the obligation of giving them a full-time or even part-time job. If you go this route, make sure you define how you're going to work together, how and when this person gets paid, and how long you expect a project to last.

Benefits of Hiring on a Contract Basis

You can mutually agree to the terms of the contract, whether for a project or ongoing help.

You pay a contractor like a supplier. The contractor gives you invoices that you pay according to the terms of your agreement. Be sure you explicitly agree to payment terms before you start the engagement.

You'll save money because you won't be paying any benefits. No vacation days, sick days, employee health benefits, etc. If they work from home, you don't have to supply them with office space.

You can end the contract at any time for any reason. You may have to give the contractor notice if that's what you've agreed.

Many freelancers like working on a contract basis because it gives them greater security. They can count on specific income over a period of time, like an employee. Depending on the contract, they may still have time to work for other clients.

Disadvantages of a Contract Relationship

Most of the disadvantages of a contractual relationship are due to its more casual nature.

Depending on the type of contract, it's likely that the contractor is also working for others. That means you have to respect their time requirements. You need to give them substantial advance notice when you'd like them to work with you so they can manage their schedule.

Even with advance notice, you may find they're not available because they're working on a big project for someone else. Some contractors or freelancers just work when it suits them. They may work for a while and then decide to travel for a few months, not taking on any work.

If you're planning to run your business primarily with contractors, you'll need to develop relationships with a few so that one can step in if your favorite isn't available. You have to plan to manage these relationships.

Benefits of Hiring Someone Part-Time

When you hire someone part-time, you're making a firmer commitment. You may decide you want someone for half days all week. Or you want a bookkeeper who comes in every Friday.

There are many potential arrangements, but there are two essential issues to consider. Like contractors, part-time workers are likely also working for someone else. So, you'll have to respect their requirements and negotiate if you need them for any additional time.

Second, talk to your accountant about the regulations and obligations of hiring someone part-time. You want this to be a contractor relationship, not a full-time employment agreement. You have to check this in your jurisdiction. Regulations vary, so be sure to look into it.

The difference generally revolves around benefits, withholding taxes, vacations, sick days, and so on.

You can end this arrangement, but because you've made a greater commitment, you'll have to give notice. You may have this in a contract, or you'll simply do it because it's the decent thing to do.

Disadvantages of Hiring Part-Time

Hiring someone part-time is very similar to working with contractors, except that you will have committed a specific amount of their time, so you have an obligation.

Let's say you have someone coming in every morning. All of a sudden, you're not so busy for a while. Depending on your agreement, you may still have to pay them. Maybe you'll have to find something else for them to do.

If you think you're not going to need them for a while, you might want to negotiate to suspend your agreement until things pick up. However, you may risk losing them altogether.

Before You Hire Anyone on Contract Basis or Part-Time, Get It in Writing

If you're hiring someone on contract or part-time, you need a written agreement before they start. Maybe you think this is too formal for your situation. It's not. A written contract is an absolute necessity.

You can find standard agreements online and customize them to suit your situation. You may want to consult with a lawyer to ensure that the contract is sufficient for your situation and the laws where you live.

Presenting a written contract may bring up some questions. That's fine—it's good to get them answered now rather than later.

For contract or part-time workers, the document should outline:

- What they're being hired for—a description of the project(s), their role.
- The expected duration of the contract, whether it's for one small project or a longer commitment, with a start date and end date, if appropriate.
- How much they're being paid.
- How frequently they will invoice you and when they get paid—every two weeks, every month, end of the project.
- Amount of notice you will give each other should either of you decide not to continue—this is more applicable for part-time hires.
- Confidentiality Agreement—you can find samples of these online too.

You should both review and sign the agreement with a copy for each of you.

At some point, if you continue to hire, you'll want templates of these types of contracts that you can quickly customize as needed.

A Caution on Contract Hires

Even though you and a contractor may be clear on your relationship with each other, the government's tax department may see it differently. Governments have many rules and regulations as to what constitutes a contract relationship versus an employee arrangement.

In some jurisdictions, you can't hire someone full-time on a contract basis for a continuous period. Or, you're limited over how much control you have over a contractor.

The reason for this is that governments would rather that you hire them as an employee, deduct and remit their income taxes as you do for all employees, and pay the contributions toward employment insurance and pension plans.

Since these regulations vary by region and country, consult with your accountant before entering into contractual arrangements to ensure you're on the right side of tax department regulations.

You do not want to be in a position of arguing with the tax department. They have endless lawyers; you do not.

Contractors, Part-Time Employees, and Your Clients

When you bring contract or part-time staff onto a project, they become part of your team. They report to your project managers the same as your employees.

So, how does this work with clients and client meetings? In my companies, we were always very upfront with clients, letting them know that they were part of our team, generally for their particular expertise.

We were never afraid that the client might try to hire them directly or question us about why they weren't on staff.

In general, clients don't care. They're happy that you've assembled an expert team to deliver their project successfully. We wanted critical team members, including contractors, in client meetings to ask questions and hear from the client directly to prevent any miscommunication later.

For example, we had a contract developer that we used on several projects. In client meetings, he would ask questions that we wouldn't have considered. He was already thinking through his options for programming, and the answers would help guide his direction.

To us, it made sense to get the right people together to shorten any lines of communication.

Benefits of Hiring Someone Full-Time

Congratulations! A full-time hire means you're building a team. You'll probably always remember your first full-time hire (Hi Aldous!), so choose carefully.

A full-time hire means they're an employee, and you're the employer. Of course, finding the right person is critical. Assuming both you and the employee are happy with the situation, you should be able to work together efficiently.

And although you're not there to be best buddies in an employer/employee relationship, ideally, you'll be able to count on each other and back each other up.

For both parties, a full-time commitment feels different than contract or freelance arrangements. You'll be closer, and spend more time together, often thinking about improving the company as it grows.

As an employer, you may choose to introduce your employee to clients. For the employee, it's a happy announcement on LinkedIn and other social platforms.

Hiring Full-Time—The Contract Becomes a Letter of Employment

If you're hiring someone full-time, your agreement becomes a letter of employment and needs to include everything in the contract agreement, plus:

- Company policy on paid holidays, vacation days, sick days, maternity leave. You'll want to ensure you're following applicable laws in your jurisdiction.
- Any other benefits which may include health care, allowances, support for ongoing education, conferences.
- A critical clause that states that the first three months are a review period, at the end of which you will meet to assess whether expectations are being met and whether the employment will continue. Be sure to go over this and discuss it explicitly.

Have two copies of the letter signed—one for you and one for them.

How to Manage Working in Different Locations

It has never been easier to have contractors or full-time employees working in different locations within your city, country, or anywhere on earth. The pandemic accelerated this trend to where it became a normal way to work.

Some companies manage this arrangement very well. For years, larger IT firms have outsourced programming and related tasks to countries such as India.

Now, with various outsourcing platforms, you can put up your projects for bids and choose the vendor who gives you the best response. If you find someone who meets your quality standards and budgets, you can continue working with them.

You can also find full-time employees that way. There are a few critical aspects of this arrangement to be considered:

1. You need processes and software to manage the relationships, especially if you're dealing with radically different time zones from your own.
2. You may have to schedule very early morning or late evening time slots if you want to have live conversations or be willing to communicate over various online platforms or email.
3. If this is a full-time employee, check to clarify their tax status and how you handle it in your bookkeeping.
4. From a company culture and morale perspective, experience shows that long-distance employees or contractors don't feel the same connection to their work as on-location staff. They don't get the benefit of regular face-to-face interactions.
5. Simultaneously, your on-location staff may not bond with the virtual team in the same way as they do with other colleagues. Take that into consideration if you plan to work this way.

Thinking of Taking on One or More Partners?

Partnerships are tricky, and you should consider them carefully before you jump in.

To begin, you should be clear why you're taking on a partner. Do you want someone to share your business with? If so, why? Is it because they bring something to the company that you couldn't get another way? Do you want to split management responsibilities with them?

The good news is that with a partner, you have an equal to talk to, someone who will either take care of the work you don't like doing or complement your creative services. They will also take on some of the responsibilities for growing and managing the company.

With more than one person, you're starting to look more like a company too. Just make sure you get along with your partner and that both of you see the business the same way. You will be spending a lot of time together, so it had better work.

Also, now you'll have two salaries to pay. Can the business support two full-time equal wages? And what about the working space? Will you have to get an office of some sort, or will you work in different spaces communicating online? Anything is possible.

Before you jump into a partnership, take time to reflect. Think about how you work best. Some people like to be the sole decision-maker and don't necessarily want to share that or have someone else weigh in.

Others work best in a team. Once you have a partner, you've committed to some degree to a team. Maybe just a team of two, but a team nonetheless.

Taking on a Partner? Consider This…

First, you need to decide whether it's an equal partnership. That means the shares of the company—yes, even private corporations have shares—would be divided 50/50, and any profits would also be divided the same way.

It doesn't have to be that way, though. One person could be bringing much more into the partnership than the other, and therefore the shares could be, say, 75/25.

But whichever way you choose to divide the shares and any money related to those shares—salaries, bonuses—the most significant challenge with partnerships is decision-making.

For example, let's assume one of you wants to hire another person, and the other isn't so sure. Or one of you wants to invest in new equipment, and the other would rather wait. Or one of you would like to declare a bonus and take some money out of the company, while the other would rather leave the money in the company.

If there are two of you, and you have equal votes, there's only one way, and that is, the decision has to be unanimous. Even if the shares are 75/25, significant decisions should still be unanimous because otherwise, one person will always overrule the other, and over time, that will ruin the partnership.

This is worth having a few in-depth discussions before you formalize a partnership. If two people are in harmony, then unanimous decisions come quickly. But if they have different objectives, dissimilar worldviews, or radically different political views, it could become a very contentious partnership.

More Than One Partner?

Some companies have many partners. If your company gets to that stage, you'll need to have a good handle on how the partnership is structured.

Get advice before taking these steps. There are many partnership models to consider.

For example, big law firms have well-established structures that often incorporate different levels of partnerships—senior partner, junior partner. The senior partners are the decision-makers; junior partners are not. When it comes to profit-sharing time, senior partners get a bigger share than junior partners. If the company is sold, senior partners benefit more than junior partners.

All of this needs to be carefully worked out. Many companies fall into serious turmoil because of disagreements on partner roles, responsibilities, and compensation. Large partner groups can complicate matters.

Also, keep in mind that if you are the company founder, every time you take on a partner, you're diluting your share of the company. That will figure into your profit sharing and your percentage of the payout if your company ever gets acquired.

For example, imagine that you're the sole owner and there's a profit of $250,000 at the end of the year. You could take it out of the company, and it would be yours alone. With one equal partner, your share is $125,000. If you have two equal partners, your share is $83,333.

You should only have multiple partners if they will help your company grow exponentially. If your partners can help build a $1 million company into a very profitable $10 million company, then it's justifiable.

To go back to the Jeff Bezos decision-making model, a partnership is a one-way door. It's complicated and usually expensive to undo, so think carefully.

You'll Need a Partnership Agreement

Once you take on a formal partner, you'll need a partnership agreement. There are many templates for these agreements available, and all of them can be customized to your situation.

Since these agreements are legal documents, I strongly advise that you and your partner sit with a lawyer to review the agreement sentence by sentence. This is the time to ask any questions about the meaning of phrases and clauses in the agreement.

Many lawyers will recommend that you each have your own lawyer. This may seem like good advice, and perhaps it's a lawyer's duty to tell you this.

But I've found that this can potentially get very contentious. You both want to agree on the terms of this document, not fight each other or contest terms. If you're already fighting at this stage, it's probably a sign that this partnership isn't such a great idea.

Ideally, both of you will have reviewed the document in advance and agreed to the terms before seeing a lawyer. Both of you should be there to ensure you understand all of the agreement's critical phrases and their implications.

Both partners have to sign off on the agreement. Keep in mind that this document will be the reference should there be any significant arguments or separations in the business.

Offering Partnerships to Employees

In some businesses, such as law firms, offering partnerships to employees is a customary way to work. Lawyers join a large firm, and if they perform well and meet management's expectations, they "make partner," generally becoming a junior partner.

If they stay around long enough, grow their business profitably, and the company has the bandwidth, they become a senior partner.

But that doesn't necessarily translate well to the creative agency business. I have known creative agencies where employees were offered partnerships. But too often, it seemed to be for the wrong reason, or the partnership was only vaguely defined.

If an employee asks about becoming a partner, you have to stop and think hard about it. Remember that when you make someone a partner, they would typically have a role in the company's management. Do you want that? Is this a person you want making business decisions with you?

You also have to wonder whether the person asking really wants that. Perhaps they think that if they were a partner, they'd make more money but haven't thought through the potential management responsibilities.

If it's a matter of someone wanting more money, you can always give them a bonus if you feel it's warranted, but let them stay an employee. Perhaps having a different title might be appropriate.

For example, they could be an associate creative director or a vice-president, but not a partner. Also, consider that once you make one person a partner, what does that mean for any other staff? Are there others who would expect to become partners?

If one of your staff suggests to you that if you don't make them a partner, they will leave the company, I would say they've already made the decision for you. As the owner, you don't want to cave in to these types of demands.

In general, I wouldn't offer partnerships to employees. It can be tough to undo if it doesn't work out. Of course, like anything else, there may be exceptions.

A Quick Story About Partnerships

When I started my first company, I knew that as a writer, I wanted a design partner.

That way, we could take care of complete projects rather than me finding a freelance designer for every project or having the client pair me with a designer. The team structure—in my case, writer and art director—is what I was comfortable with when I worked in ad agencies.

I also wanted someone who had experience running a company and had their own freelance business. I was looking for a partner who had some management experience so that we would share those responsibilities.

I put an ad in an industry publication, got about 30 responses, talked to five of them, and eventually chose the one I thought would work out best. We had a few meetings to see how we got along, what business we could bring to the partnership and how we would operate. We decided to work on a few jobs together before formalizing anything.

Everything went well, and we agreed to form the company together as equal partners. However, before we did that, I had some questions about how to split the money.

In those days, designers could make quite a bit of income beyond the design fees by handling the printing and marking it up. Let's say a design job was $5,000. A big print run could cost $50,000. Marking it up by just 15 percent would mean another $7,500.

So, should my design partner also split the $7,500 with me? How would that work?

At that time, I had an accountant who we agreed we would use for our company. He specialized in working with creative agencies and was terrific at advising young companies. My partner and I went to see him.

His advice was simple and straightforward. Be 50/50 partners in everything. Both of you will be working hard to launch the company and making it a success.

One day, one of you will bring in more money, the next day, it will be the other guy. Don't dissect every dollar. Talk to each other far before you want to make any significant decisions, so neither of you is wholly set in your position when it comes time to decide. Be flexible. Do what's best for the company.

That advice served us well. Business is complicated enough without having intricate decision-making processes or splitting the money in weird ways.

Should Your Spouse be a Partner?

For some people, this becomes the most personal business decision they'll ever have to make. I've seen it work fantastically and also disastrously. Assuming your spouse wants to work with you in your business, here are a few things to consider:

- You'll be together 24/7. Your whole life will become your business. Are you both okay with that?
- You'll both share the worries and concerns of the business. Neither can act as a relief for the other.
- If you have other staff, it can be strange for them to work for a couple. Employees won't be comfortable coming to one of you to talk about the other. Similarly, if you have other partners, they may feel that the two of you will always agree in decision-making (whether that's true or not), to their disadvantage.
- What about vacations? You'll want to go together. How does that work for the rest of the company?

- And, critically, how's your marriage or civil partnership? What would happen to the company if you decided to separate or divorce? You should make provisions for all outcomes before signing legal partnership agreements.

This decision is highly individual and one you'll have to make for yourselves. You may also want some tax planning advice, but after that, it's up to you.

Last Word on Partnerships

Be extremely careful taking on a partner. Do your due diligence, and take your time. Work together for a while before formalizing an agreement.

You might also look at other arrangements for working together. For example, you could agree to profit sharing (it doesn't have to be 50/50) without making another person a partner.

Understand that partnerships are not meant to last forever. At some point, partners will want to leave for various reasons.

Therefore, your partnership agreement must include a definite process for undoing the partnership. If one partner decides to leave, they have to sell their shares back to the company. What's the agreed-upon arrangement for that process?

There are many horror stories about partnerships coming undone—ugly divorces, rip-offs, and huge disappointments. Go into any partnership with your eyes wide open.

Chapter Takeaways

- You should think hard anytime you're contemplating bringing on more people, whether it's contract, part-time, full-time, or partner.

- The higher the commitment—a full-time hire or a partner—the more critical the decision. A mistake here can be expensive and cause significant damage to your company.
- The stakes are even higher if you decide to make your spouse a partner in the company.
- Take some time with your partnership agreement. Make sure it works for all involved.
- Try to keep financial agreements within the partnership as simple as possible. Complex agreements only create more work for lawyers.

20

MANAGING EMPLOYEES AND BENEFITS

"On a team, sometimes you just need a manager who cares about you."

— Mario Maruffi

Do You Need an Employee Handbook?

Creating an employee handbook isn't an immediate concern when you're starting but becomes a good idea once you grow past a few employees.

The handbook sets out the company's vision, code of conduct, benefits, and general housekeeping rules. It helps employees understand your expectations of them.

We found it useful in our onboarding. We'd review it with new employees and give them an opportunity to ask any questions.

Here's an outline of the sections you'd typically find in an employee handbook:

- Company mission

- Code of conduct
- Organization chart
- Job descriptions
- Reviews
- Holidays, vacation, sick days, maternity leave
- Health benefits plan
- A typical letter of employment
- Confidentiality agreement

Talking to Employees About Money

When you first hire an employee, you agree on salary and benefits. But often left unsaid are reviews and raises. Employees expect to get some kind of raise in pay after a period of employment. They also want feedback on their performance.

Here's what I suggest:

When you first hire someone, let them know that you will review their salary annually. Make sure that you or the office manager marks the date in a calendar. You can be sure that the employee will be very aware of the date and will expect a meeting to discuss their performance and salary.

Also, by letting them know that it's an annual review, they won't come to you before to discuss their salary.

Don't mention or indicate the amount of a typical raise, especially during the hiring meeting. This should be entirely up to you, based on the employee's performance and their value to the company.

In terms of feedback, provide it as you work together. If you're happy with something they've done, let them know. If they're exceeding your expectations, tell them.

On the other hand, if you're unhappy, and you want to see changes in how they work, tell them that too. There's no need to hold it back for an annual review. Imagine you're the employee for a moment. You don't want to find out after a year that your boss is dissatisfied with your work.

Most employees want to work in a way that makes you happy. They want to know they're living up to expectations. Many of them crave feedback. Give it to them.

Before the anniversary, set up a date and time to meet. You may want to put your comments in writing to help you remember. It's up to you. In any case, you need to be prepared with what you want to say about their performance and what you're offering for a raise.

You will get one of three reactions to your comments and your offer:

1. They may be delighted, and thank you.
2. They may not say much and be accepting of it.
3. Or they may let you know they expected more. In advance, you'll need to think about how you want to handle any potential disappointment.

You should also not be surprised if an employee decides to leave your company after a performance review. Perhaps they've been thinking of moving on but waited until they learned of the amount of the raise. This is predictable, especially after they've been with you for a few years.

Employees sometimes use these meetings to evaluate their worth in the market. If they've been making $65,000 and you offer them a raise to $72,000, they'll go out on interviews asking for $80,000. And really, you can't blame them. You may have done the same in the past.

Holiday Bonuses—Yes or No?

There is a tradition of the "Christmas bonus" in many companies. It's up to you whether you want to follow it.

In my companies, we gave holiday bonuses. The amounts were arbitrary. Depending on how good the previous year was, we would create a bonus pool as a percentage of profit and then decide how to allocate it.

We didn't explain or justify it to anyone. We simply gave each employee a season's greetings card with a friendly note and a check. We based the bonus on our feelings about their performance and contribution to the company over the previous year.

Our accountant had a different view. He didn't believe in these types of bonuses. Why? He argued that once you start giving them, they become expected. What if you have a downturn in business and aren't in a position to give bonuses? He felt that salaries and benefits should be appropriate, and the company isn't Santa Claus.

So, take your pick. Whether or not you give these types of bonuses is an entirely individual choice.

Profit Sharing—Yes or No?

Instead of handing out holiday bonuses, some companies offer their employees profit sharing. In practice, it may amount to much of the same thing, other than timing. Any shared profits would be distributed sometime after your year-end when you've got your final numbers, rather than before the holiday season.

Out of the profits, you would typically create a pool for distribution. Standard practice is to distribute about 10 percent of the profits. Keep in mind as you're doing this that whatever you're sharing comes out of your pocket. If you chose not to share profits, you could keep more for yourself or leave it in the company.

The pros and cons are similar to holiday bonuses. Employees expect them, and they may start to count on them, which could backfire if there are fewer profits to share. They may not be satisfied with the amount even in a good year.

In my companies, we chose a holiday bonus rather than profit sharing. Everyone is happy to get more money right before the holidays. You can decide whether you want to do either, or none at all.

Consider How You Handle Holidays, Sick Days, Maternity Leave, and Other Time Off

In your employee handbook, your letters of employment, or any other agreement you make with someone working for you, you'll need to address how your company pays for holidays, sick days, maternity leave, jury duty, time off to vote in elections, funerals, and other types of time off.

In the U.S., there is no legal requirement to pay for any of these. In fact, there is no legal requirement for employers to give employees any vacation, paid or not. Surprised? The minimum requirements are extremely low and are all up to the employer.

Most other countries have more generous requirements for employees. In Canada, for example, you are obligated to give two weeks of paid time off after the first year of employment. After five years, it's three weeks, and after ten years, it's four weeks.

Important: If you're an American company and try to follow the "you don't have to pay for anything" guidelines, you'll have no employees. The creative services industry is somewhat more enlightened than others, and no one would stand for a path of servitude.

It's worth talking to a Human Resources consultant to better understand typical benefits. Also, if you've worked at companies that are similar to the one you're starting, think back on the benefits you received there. Would they be a basis for what you would offer?

You can decide how detailed you want to get in your handbook descriptions and how much you're willing to wait until issues come up before developing policies for them.

However, once you make any kind of agreement with your employees about benefits, you are obligated to live up to them.

For example, can employees accumulate vacation time over years, or must the vacation time be used each calendar year? Does an employee have the choice of not taking the vacation but getting paid for it? What if they want to take half their vacation but be paid for the other half?

My recommendation is to get the basics into any agreement or employee handbook and deal with special requests as they come. If you haven't written out how you will address any requests outside of the basics, then you have the option of handling them on a case-by-case basis.

Try to be reasonable and keep the employee happy, but don't turn the whole world upside down to accommodate requests.

In my companies, we provided vacation as stipulated, and we paid jury duty days, time to attend funerals, and other necessary time off. Canada has a prescribed way to handle maternity leave through government benefits, which we followed.

Encourage Employees to Use Their Vacation Time

According to the U.S. Travel Association, more than half of Americans who get paid vacation don't take all of it, or in some cases, any of it. Those who do often work while they should be vacationing.[1] Furthermore, many company cultures discourage employees from going on vacation.

Don't be like that. Encourage people to use their vacation time and insist that they unplug from work while away. Organize the company around that value. People in the creative agency business need time to recharge and think different thoughts rather than work or worry about client work.

However, you do have to schedule vacations, and employees need to give ample notice when they want to take their time. As an employer, you have the right to deny specific days because others are also away at the same time. You can't have your whole design department on vacation at the same time. Use a vacation calendar to manage that.

Working Hours and Overtime for Full-Time Employees

This next section applies to companies where full-time employees work out of the same office. In other words, something like a traditional 9-5 arrangement.

These days, many companies have a core group that works out of an office, augmented by employees, contractors, or suppliers who may be anywhere in the world. This section is about you and your core group.

If it's your company, and you love what you do, you're probably spending long hours at the office. There's always something that needs to be done, whether it's client work, company admin chores, new business pitches—the work never seems to go away.

It's your baby, and you knew when you started that extended hours would be part of the job. So, it's tempting to think that your employees feel the same way.

You may be surprised to learn that generally, they don't. For them working at your company is a job. They get paid to work during regular work hours. They have a life outside of their job and look forward to their own time.

But what happens when you need them to work a bit longer to finish off a project, or even to work over a weekend?

Address Overtime Work in the Letter of Employment

The time to agree on how you will handle overtime is before you hire an employee. But, keep in mind, there are laws governing overtime and an employer's obligation to compensate.

As an owner, you need to understand the details of these laws as they apply to your jurisdiction. For example, in some states and provinces, a workweek is defined as 40 hours. In other jurisdictions, it's 48 hours. Laws may require a specific payment, typically time and a half, for any hours over the defined workweek.

I can already hear you say, "Wait, that's not how we work at all. Nobody gets paid by the hour here, and we don't track overtime like that. It's more flexible than that. We give them time off to make up for it..."

In most cases, you can make whatever arrangements you and your employees agree upon to compensate for overtime work. However, you should check to be sure that you're following the law in your area.

The key to your overtime arrangement is, it must be in writing. Whether you pay them (you can work out an hourly wage based on their salary) or give them extra time off, it should be a written agreement.

Whatever you agree to should be spelled out in your letter of employment that the employees signed. Employees must expressly agree to the overtime arrangement.

If you decide, like many creative agencies do, that you will give time off for any overtime, at a minimum, you have to give an hour and a half for every hour worked. So, if someone stays for two hours, you need to calculate three hours off.

Whatever your arrangement is, make sure it's within the law of your jurisdiction, and it's in writing, explicit, and upfront.

Time Off for Overtime Work Should Be Taken Sooner Rather Than Later

Ideally, you want the employee to take their time off relatively soon after they worked overtime. Not surprisingly, you'll find Friday afternoons (or all day, depending on the number of hours) to be popular choices.

You should agree to that as soon as possible. You generally don't want to "bank" the hours so that employees end up taking multiple days or weeks at a time. It's just one more thing for you to keep track of and work around.

We always encouraged the employee to take the time within a week or two. They gave you the time, you give it back to them, and both move on, with no complicated tracking needed.

Not Every Employee Can Work Overtime

Here's another reason to agree on overtime work upfront so that you're not surprised later. Some employees will have young children at day care or other reasons they can't work overtime. They have to get out right at 5:00 or whatever you set as the end of the day.

Overtime work is impossible or challenging for them. Or they catch a train home, and if they leave too late, they miss the usual train and may be delayed by hours before the next one.

Even if employees agreed to terms of compensation for overtime work, it doesn't mean they will do it. All kinds of situations affect a person's working hours. As an employer, you have to be sensitive to them to ensure you're abiding by the laws and keeping your employee happy.

You Can't Force Someone to Work Overtime

It's up to the employee to agree to work the extra hours. If they can't, or simply don't want to, there's little you can do about it.

It's against the law virtually everywhere to try to force someone or in any way punish them for not working beyond their regular work hours. That's why open communication, well ahead of time, is essential.

For example, if a group of you are working on a presentation for Friday morning, you may know from experience that you'll be there late Thursday night to finish up the last details. It's predictable.

So ideally, you should talk to your employees early in the week to check whether they'll be able to stay later on Thursday to help. Don't leave it until the last minute. They may be happy to stay, but they need to make arrangements ahead of time.

What About Flexible Hours?

Some of your employees may propose to work somewhat different hours than everyone else. For example, I've had employees who just can't get up early in the morning, so they wanted to work closer to 10:00–6:00 or 11:00–7:00, rather than 9:00–5:00.

Anything is possible as long as it suits both parties. On both sides, you need consistency and predictability. You need to know when they're available for work, and they need to know that they have a commitment to you for a predetermined period.

I wouldn't advise you to stretch the bounds of your regular hours too far. What if someone wants to work just nights, but not days? How would that affect your ability to work together? Again, it's okay if it works for both of you.

Note that this is a different situation from working with a contractor or supplier, where you brief them, and they do the work on their own time, as long as it meets your deadlines.

For example, I've had contractors programming websites while working from home in different time zones. We never met except on chat, and there was no expectation that we would work from the same space or that they would work during specific hours.

Your Employees Aren't On Call 24/7

Just because you have your employees' phone numbers doesn't mean you can call or text them at all hours of the day. Your employees are "on the clock" during agreed-upon working hours. If you need to get in touch outside of those hours, it should be only in an emergency.

The same goes for emails. Something may pop into your head late at night that you want to share with one or more employees. Make yourself a note and share it when the next workday starts. Or write the email and schedule when it's to be sent. You're not expecting them to do anything about it overnight, are you?

A general rule might be the 7-to-7 rule. All communications happen between seven in the morning and seven in the evening, not before or after.

Now, if you're working with a contractor in a different time zone, say programmers in India, they're accustomed to getting messages from their clients around the world at all hours and will respond when it's their work time.

But for someone in your city and time zone, keep the communications to working hours. They agreed to work for you, not to be on call around the clock.

Non-Compete Clauses

Sometimes people think of non-compete clauses in conjunction with confidentiality agreements. They're distantly related, but not the same thing.

A non-compete clause prevents an employee leaving your company from working with a competitor (however that's defined) for a period of time, typically two or three years.

Non-compete clauses in creative agencies are very unusual and generally unenforceable. They amount to denying someone the right to work in their industry.

These clauses are more enforceable in large companies where high-level executives have left, often with a bundle of cash in a severance agreement. They are prohibited from working in that industry or with a direct competitor for a few years. However, the money they left with more than equals what they would make during the forced unemployment.

So, unless you're willing to pay a significant severance fee, and the employee or partner leaving agrees to it, you can generally forget about non-compete clauses.

Think About "Soft Benefits" for Your Employees

In running a creative agency, I never wanted to be "best friends" with employees, but encouraged a friendly work atmosphere.

So, I'd say no to one-on-one, let's go out for a beer, but yes to soft benefits for all employees.

For example, since we knew everyone's birthday, we would have a birthday cake celebration in the boardroom. We usually did it mid-afternoon to give everyone a little break, stand around, embarrass them (and ourselves) by singing Happy Birthday, chat, and eat cake.

We also had staff parties in restaurants, one in the summer, another before Christmas. We'd have some suggestions for restaurants, would ask staff for ideas, and then would pick one. We'd usually start it as a late lunch, and it would last the afternoon.

During July and August, we'd have summer Fridays. The staff could take Friday afternoon off, assuming there were no pressing deadlines they had to meet. We tried to make sure everyone could take advantage of it.

If someone worked especially hard on a project that involved overtime, not only did we give them the appropriate time off to compensate, but we often would give them a restaurant gift voucher for two as a thank you.

For a while, we had a candy dish. Close to our office, there was a fantastic candy store. Unfortunately, we had to put an end to that after discovering our office admin had managed to open a corporate account there. We were spending over $150 a week on Jujubes and other candy!

We replaced it with a fruit bowl.

Chapter Takeaways

- If this is the first time you're in charge of employees, it will be a learning curve for you to manage.
- An employee handbook is a good idea. It forces you to formulate how you want to deal with employees, it standardizes what you want to say, and saves you time from going over it. It's also a useful reference for employees.
- When it comes to vacation time, holidays, etc., make sure that, at the very least, you comply with the law. You may choose to be more generous than the minimum.
- Respect your employees' time. They have a life away from the office.
- Think about soft benefits that are fun for your employees and you can afford. (Maybe not $150 a week on candy.)

---

1. "Study: A Record 768 Million U.S. Vacation Days Went unused in '18, Opportunity Cost in the Billions," *U.S. Travel Association*, August 16, 2019. https://www.ustravel.org/press/study-record-768-million-us-vacation-days-wetmnt-unused-18-opportunity-cost-billions.

21

TAKE TIME SHEETS SERIOUSLY

"They always say time changes things, but you actually have to change them yourself."

— Andy Warhol

The Discipline of Time Management and Time Sheets

I can already hear the whining. Time sheets? You must be kidding! Go away!

Bear with me... I know that most creative people wish time sheets didn't exist. Doing time sheets feels like accounting, and if we had wanted to be accountants, we would have gone to accounting school.

However, from a business perspective, accurate time sheets are a must. There's no way around it. But remember, they're only a record of how jobs were done. Time sheets record history. What you have to master at the outset is time management for both yourself and your employees.

For any project, you'll break it down by deliverables and assign people to each deliverable. You may do this on your own or work together with a project manager. To come up with the estimate, you have to decide how much time you're allocating per person per deliverable.

Ideally, you should speak to the people you've assigned and let them know how much time you've allocated for them to complete their tasks.

You may get some pushback. They may say, "I can't do that in just three hours. I need at least a whole day." In that case, your options are to add to the hours, assign it to someone else, or help the person with the assignment so they can do it more efficiently.

After a while, having done several similar projects, you should have a good feeling for how much time to give to each task. Part of time management involves thorough briefings, providing direction, and clear expectations.

You should also ensure that the person doing the task can dedicate the time to it without unnecessary interruptions. If you have someone working on a deadline for you, you can't interrupt them with something else.

You also want enough discipline in the studio so that employees aren't interrupting each other. It's normal to have some chatter first thing in the morning and around lunch, but once staff are focused on their work, they should be left alone to do it.

Be aware of anyone who likes to be on their phone talking or texting all day with friends or other employees. It can be very disruptive and needs to stop. Studies show that, on average, it takes 25 minutes for a person to get back on track after an interruption.[1] Yikes!

Looking at your time estimates sometimes requires a gut check. Are the hours you want to allocate to a task reasonable for what needs to be done?

If you find that you're getting constant pushback from employees about not having enough time for the job, you'll need to examine what changes you need to make. Maybe you're unreasonable in your assumptions, but perhaps not.

In general, staff have to understand where the revenue comes from and the need to work efficiently. As their leader, you need to get a handle on your staff's capabilities to ensure you have the right people to complete the projects within the allocated time.

I know that some business owners have trouble with this idea. They believe that you can't rush creativity. They may be concerned that they won't get the best creative solutions due to time pressure. They might feel that they're coming down too hard on their employees.

Nonsense. Having deadlines and discipline stimulates thinking. It's the same endorphins that kick in during any competitive game or quest. Football, basketball, and hockey players know that they're playing against the clock. They need to score their points before time runs out.

When there is a defined goal, people rise to the occasion.

Get Real About Time Sheet Data

Wouldn't it be great if all of your employee time were 100 percent billable? Every minute, every hour, billed to clients.

It's not. Not even close. You have tasks that are not billable to projects. That includes creating estimates and invoices, answering RFPs, doing internal work such as updating your website and portfolio, making social media posts, and entering awards shows, among other things.

As a rule of thumb, your overall billable efficiency for all staff, including those who aren't billable (e.g., bookkeepers), should be between 50 percent and 75 percent of all available hours.

That means that if you took all the working hours in a month, multiply that by the total number of staff and multiply that by your billing rate, you should be billing between 50 and 75 percent of that total.

If it's toward the bottom of that, you should be looking for ways to improve it. That means your company isn't working efficiently or you don't have enough work. If it's much above 75 percent, it's either unrealistic, or you're ignoring internal work that should be done.

Here's another way to look at it. If you break out staff who should be doing billable client work, in other words, writers, designers, and project managers (don't count admin assistants, or your bookkeeper, etc.), their billable rate should be around 80 percent of their time. If it's much below that, you need to investigate.

Why might it be lower? You're not busy enough, so they have nothing to do. They've been given tasks that could be done by someone else—generally a lower-paid administrative person. They're goofing off when they should be working. Perhaps they're not keeping accurate time sheets.

Have a look and see what's in the time sheets.

Working Hours, Billing Rates, and the Value of Efficiency

As a rule of thumb, here's how you calculate working hours in a year:

Assume 40 hours a week x 52 weeks = 2,080 hours

From that, subtract two weeks vacation (80 hours), about 10 statutory holidays (80 hours), and, on average, three sick days (24 hours).

That totals 1,896 hours. For senior staff who take more than two weeks of vacation, there will be fewer hours. If you decide to close the office between Christmas and New Year's, or if you have a staff retreat, you'll have to subtract those hours, too.

Do the calculations for your staff and office and use that as a basis for calculating billable efficiency.

Here's the fastest, most uncomplicated calculation you can do to see whether you're billing approximately what you should be.

Take the number of billable hours in your year—let's round it down to 1,800—multiply that by the number of full-time staff, by your billing rate, then by 60 percent billable efficiency (or pick a number between 50 percent and 75 percent).

To make the math easy for this example, let's say you have a total staff of 10. That should give you your reasonable annual billing number.

When you first run these formulas, you're guessing at your billable efficiency. Do a calculation and compare it against what you have billed. After a few calculations, you'll figure out your current billable efficiency.

So, the formula is: 1,800 hours, x 10 staff x $150 billing rate x .6 billable efficiency.

Let's look at the difference your billing rate makes:

At a billing rate of $150, it would be 1,800 x 10 x $150 x .6 = $1,620,000.

Make the billing rate $175, and it's $1,890,000.

Make the billing rate $200, and it's $2,160,000.

So, the same number of staff, same billable efficiency, but higher billing rates. A difference of over $500,000 per year.

But let's say you can't raise your billing rate. How about improving your billable efficiency? Let's take a look at the same billing rate of $150, but see the effect of billable efficiency on your potential revenue.

If you take a billing rate of $150:

At 50 percent efficiency, it's $1,350,000

At 60 percent efficiency, it's $1,620,000

At 75 percent efficiency, it's $2,025,000

The same number of people, the same number of hours, the same billing rate. The only difference is how efficiently you can operate your company. That's a spread of nearly $700,000 a year between the top and the bottom. It's all pure profit.

Now imagine you were fully optimized: you have your highest billing rate, let's say $200 (could be higher), and you're working at 75 percent efficiency. Your potential revenue would be $2,700,000.

That happens to be exactly twice as much as the lowest billing rate at the lowest efficiency. Most of it is profit. You might consider bonuses as an incentive to employees to work as efficiently as possible.

Take a moment to study these numbers to truly appreciate the difference your billing rate and billable efficiency makes. See where you can best maximize your billings, assuming, of course, that you have enough work to keep everyone busy.

If you don't want to do these financial exercises, find someone in your company to do them for you. It could be your bookkeeper or a project manager. Set up some formulas in a spreadsheet and run the numbers.

You may also want to review with your accountant. The accountant could give you an outside perspective with insights into how companies similar to yours are performing.

Conclusion: You Have Greatest Control Over Operating Efficiency

Go back and review the numbers in the previous section. Think about where you can benefit the most. Generally, you can't raise your rates indefinitely (although you could probably raise them a bit each year).

Realistically, you can't increase the number of working hours. You could hire more employees, but of course only if you have work for them.

Your most significant opportunity to increase revenue is by working more efficiently. What does that mean? To operate efficiently, you:

- Have defined processes for how the agency performs most common tasks. You don't keep reinventing the wheel. Employees know how they should be working.
- Have appropriate tools and platforms that allow you to collaborate and communicate effectively.
- Have a chain of command that works for your company. Everyone knows who they report to, who they work with on any given project.
- Have the right clients for your company. You know their businesses. You already are or are becoming experts in your niche.

It's worth taking the time, probably one or two weekend retreats, with your key team members to look at how you work.

If possible, get examples of how other creative agencies like yours function, right down to the smallest details. How do you get that information? Ask them. It's likely more straightforward than you think.

Then tear apart your current processes. Look for flaws in how you work. Find ways to fix them. Look at your team. Do you have the right people to achieve the performance levels you're targeting?

Time Sheet Rules

There are only two critical time sheet rules that everyone, including you, should abide by.

First, everyone must enter their time sheet data at the end of every day, and secondly, it must be accurate.

If you let it go for a day or two, you're creating fiction. No one remembers what they worked on two days ago and for how long they worked on it.

Someone, likely a project manager, needs to be the time sheet police. It's not a popular job, but it must be done. Staff has to understand the importance of accurate timekeeping.

Perhaps your time sheet software has an automatic notification to remind people early the next morning that their previous day's time sheet is due.

In some agencies, this is the hardest thing to enforce, and some agency owners just give up. You could forget about time sheets, but you lose any real metrics for how well your company performs. It will be tough to improve efficiency without this data.

What is the Real Reason for Time Sheets?

There's a widespread perception that time sheets are a way to police your staff to make sure they're working on projects. There's some truth to that, but if you think about it, staff will soon realize they'll get found out anyway.

Let's say you have a designer who's wasting time all day. What's he going to put on his time sheet?

If he puts the hours towards client work, it will soon become apparent that there are many hours, but little work was done. And assuming he has a deadline for delivering his work, he'll be hard-pressed to meet it.

If he puts it against an admin job, it will also become apparent that he's spending far too much time on "admin" and not on real projects.

Aside from that, you and your project managers should be aware of what staff are working on and when you expect them to finish their immediate assignment. Realistically, by the time you review time sheets, it will be ancient history anyway.

The only reason for closely monitoring employees' performance is when you have a new employee. It's worth keeping an eye on the time sheets of people new to your agency to see whether they meet your expectations for deliverables. They may be a lot faster or slower in their work than you thought.

Other than that, there are two main reasons for accurate time sheets. The first is to help you and anyone who creates estimates to get as precise as possible in your estimating.

You want someone to periodically review time sheets against estimates and invoices to see how you're doing. Are you delivering as you thought you would when you created the estimate?

This goes back to profitable clients and profitable types of projects. Only by reviewing and comparing will you specifically learn how you're doing, where you're doing well, and where you need to make some changes.

These reviews allow you to adjust and improve your estimating.

If you find yourself estimating 25 hours for a task but find 60 hours on the time sheets, you need to uncover the reason for the discrepancy.

You don't want to get into the habit of estimating 25 hours for that task on future jobs. Your goal should be to deliver projects within 10 percent of your estimate.

The second reason for keeping a close eye on time sheets is when you're introducing a new type of service or deliverable.

The first few times you sell this new service, you're guesstimating and hoping for the best. You quickly want to get some degree of accuracy to be confident you can deliver the service profitably.

You're going to want reports to review. You may find that a project manager is the best one to create these reports for you. If you can check them and be confident that they're accurate, you'll save the time it takes to compile the information.

Based on these reports, you may want to meet with key staff to review the findings and get their impressions. They may have good ideas on improving your operating efficiency and deliverables.

At some point, when you have a general staff meeting, time sheets will undoubtedly come up. This is when you should let them know why accuracy and completeness are so important.

It's not you policing them, but instead, you getting the information you need to create more accurate estimates.

You could also include a section on time sheets in your employee handbook. Have the time sheet discussion right at the hiring stage to set expectations.

Chapter Takeaways

- In the creative agency business, time is money. It's as simple as that. Pay attention to time sheets. Analyze that information and act on it to improve estimating and profitability.
- Working more efficiently is often easier than raising rates. Your ultimate goal is to have the agency working at peak efficiency, charging the highest rates that your clients will pay.
- If you don't have the patience to dig through time sheet data, find someone who does. Perhaps it's a project manager who can do the analysis and review the data with you. Ignoring this means you're flying blind.

---

1. Bob Sullivan and Hugh Thompson, "Brain, Interrupted," The *New York Times*, May 3, 2013. https://www.nytimes.com/2013/05/05/opinion/sunday/a-focus-on-distraction.html.

22

GROWING YOUR AGENCY

"Sometimes life knocks you on your ass... get up, get up, get up!!! Happiness is not the absence of problems, it's the ability to deal with them."

— Steve Maraboli

Make New Business Development a Priority

Once you have your business up and running, you should be thinking about getting more clients. There's a simple law of growth: you're either growing or shrinking—there's no such thing as standing still.

But you don't want just any clients—you want to work with companies and organizations that fit the niches you've defined for yourself. Ideally, you want clients with an ongoing demand for the services you provide rather than one-time projects.

Your first goal is to get 10 substantial clients who give you steady, profitable work throughout the year.

Generate Word of Mouth

Word of mouth and personal recommendations are still among the most powerful ways to meet new people who might be interested in your services.

When you're just launching your company, you're going to have to kick-start the word of mouth. That means telling everyone you know about your new company.

You'll want a short, friendly message that communicates your company's services. Bring it up at appropriate times. Hand out business cards.

Often, this may seem like a waste of time, and realistically, word of mouth on its own isn't much of a new business strategy.

But it's fundamental. Just remember that all the people you know —family, friends, acquaintances—all influence their circle of friends. Word gets around, and people will go to your site to see what you're doing.

Sooner or later, someone will want to talk to you about your services, or they'll say, "Hey, you should speak to my friend about this."

Also, talking about your company to people you know is good practice for getting your elevator pitch refined and answering questions that inevitably come up. Talk it up. People like to spread good news, and an entrepreneur like you with a new agency is certainly worth talking about.

Start New Business Development with the Basics—Your Website and Social Media

Your website should be your home base. No matter where else you show your work—YouTube, Instagram, Facebook, Twitter—

you want to have it prominent on your site. You own your site; you don't own any of the social media properties, and you have no control over what happens to them.

Feature the client work you're most proud of front and center on your site. Don't bury it in the navigation. Update your site with new client work regularly. Ensure you're only showing your very best samples representing the type of work you're pursuing.

Don't show anything that would lead to a direction you don't want to follow. Even if it's cool, if it's a one-off that doesn't align with your goals, leave it off the site.

What else goes on your site? Bios and good photos of your key people, an "About" section where you talk about your philosophy and the type of work and clients you specialize in.

What about blogging? If you have a writer who enjoys writing posts and will stick to blogging on a regular schedule, and if you have perspectives and insights that will benefit prospective clients, then yes.

A blog can be a powerful tool and help you build authority, word of mouth, and improve the SEO for your site—however, a word of caution. There are thousands of abandoned blogs out there. Nothing looks worse than a blog where the most recent post is years old. So, think about it. Many people find it easier to maintain an active social presence than a blog.

A tip for whoever is doing your site navigation and layout: find a spot on the home page for your phone number and address. Do you know how many times people will come to your site to find your number or figure out where to send a courier delivery? Don't bury it.

By now, it should go without saying, but design your site for mobile-first, then desktop. If you look at your stats, you'll see more and more visitors are accessing your site through mobile.

Make sure it performs well, everything is readable, and information loads in the order you expect.

Your site should incorporate SEO in the programming and writing. If you're not an SEO expert, find someone who is to make sure it starts to show up in appropriate searches. It could take some time for search engines to find you, but it will never happen without good SEO.

After your site, the next place to be prominent is on LinkedIn. You should have a company page, and your key people need full profiles. Spend some time on LinkedIn, and learn from their tutorials on making pages with impact. Then use LinkedIn to distribute news to your networks.

After that, pick the social media platforms that make sense for you and interact with them regularly. Pick your spots—you want to focus on one or two platforms.

You can't be everywhere and do it effectively, especially when you're just starting. You won't have time. You can always expand later, but it's a real waste to start something, then abandon it.

If you're in the film business, you're on YouTube and perhaps Vimeo. And given its visual nature, Instagram is a good choice for most creators.

All of this—your site and social media—is foundational. It's there so that when someone looks for you, they'll find you. It should be the best version of yourself—shiny, sparkling, optimistic, and powerful.

Don't be one of those sad people who make excuses for their site or social media presence. "It's not up to date, we're still working on it..." You should be able to give people your website and social media addresses and be confident that they represent you as you wish to be seen.

Using Social Media for Promotion

It's not a matter of whether you should use social media to promote your business (you should), but how to do it effectively.

Here are some points to consider:

- Pick a few channels where you can excel and post regularly. If you're going to have a presence, it should be lively, not a morgue of old posts.
- Figure out a strategy for the content you'll post and assign someone a schedule for posting. Brainstorm your first dozen posts so you have some momentum.
- If you're thinking video, consider how you want to use it. What do you want to say and show? Ideally, you will want to think in terms of a series so that you have a related family of videos.
- You can use YouTube as a base and post the same or edited versions to other platforms such as Facebook, Instagram, Twitter, TikTok, and LinkedIn. Focus on being interesting rather than perfect, and distribute across your platforms.
- Keeping up your social presence takes time. Don't underestimate it. This is time away from client work, not something you or your staff will do in their "spare time." (What's that?) So, take it seriously and think about your expected return on the time you've invested.
- Post something of value to your clients and potential clients. It could be new client work (get their permission first), your perspectives on marketing techniques or trends, or observations about relevant industry news. Add something personal, like a staff party, for a change of pace, but mostly stick to what will be useful for clients.
- You don't need massive followings for social media to be

successful. Better to have the right followers than thousands of bots. Don't buy followers. Ever. Build them organically.

- Use links to drive traffic from social media to your site, where you can present more detailed information. Inbound links also help your search engine rankings.
- Do not use your site to drive traffic to your social platforms. That's a mistake. You're pushing people away from you—the next thing you know, they're scrolling through Instagram and have forgotten all about you.
- Your goal is to get them to the one property you own: your website. You might consider building specific landing pages for your social media posts.
- Complete your profiles on your social media accounts. If you need some help, look at the profiles of big accounts for tips.
- Keep SEO in mind for the text in your profiles—social media shows up in search, but only if you have text for the search engines to find.
- Remember that it's called social media. Follow people and companies, especially your clients, and comment, share, like, etc. Make yourself known. DM carefully, only when you have something of value to offer that person— no social spamming! No one asked for it.
- Periodically, look at the analytics for your site and your social media platforms. Figure out what works and do more of that. If a platform doesn't work for you, either switch tactics or platforms. Don't waste time on what isn't working.
- If you're thinking of doing paid ads on social media, make sure you have the expertise to manage it. If you don't have the talent in-house, you can hire experts. Although social media can target better than any other

medium, you can waste a lot of time and money here if you don't know what you're doing.

- An Instagram tip: You only get one live URL that's in your bio. Rather than use it to link to your home page or specific article, create a page on your site that is a visual table of contents page to blog posts or pages on your website that you've promoted on Instagram. Here's why.
- Let's say you put up a new blog post every week. If you link directly to that post, you miss the opportunity to show the visitor all of your previous posts. Your visual table of contents page should be your Instagram images, each linked to the respective blog post or page. That gives you many more chances to drive traffic to all of your pages.

Promote Your Vendor of Record Status

On your website, wherever you show logos of prominent clients (and you should do that), you should also note the names of any companies and organizations where you are an approved vendor. This boosts your credibility and may help get you invited to apply for other vendor lists.

Where to Focus Personal Networking

Fish where the fish are. It sounds simple, but so many in the creative agency business don't seem to know that. They go to design conferences, where they mostly meet their peers and competition and call it networking. It doesn't work that way.

You want to spend your time where your potential clients are.

For example, we had electric utility clients. We attended electric utility conferences and secured a speaking engagement where we were able to talk about marketing trends for utilities. That introduced us to new prospects in an industry where we were marketing experts.

Whatever areas of business you work in, those are the conferences you want to attend, and if possible, be featured as a speaker.

Another example: My first job in advertising was with a company that specialized in real estate. We created ads and materials to sell condos and subdivision homes. The company owner was good at coming up with sales ideas and pitches.

At least once or twice a year, he would get himself a speaking gig at a construction or builders' conference. There were many of them, all across North America.

He'd be the only marketing person on the agenda—everyone else was selling building materials, builder's software, etc. And every time, he would come back with a pocket full of business cards and at least one or two new clients.

He also used the opportunity to reconnect with existing clients. The big builders always had new projects in the pipeline, and he wanted to make sure that he would get the marketing campaigns for those projects.

Whether or not you speak at these events, this is where you should be making new contacts.

Have an elevator pitch prepared so that when you get the inevitable question, "What do you do?" you'll have a polished, friendly answer. You should be able to deliver it in one sentence. Don't start rambling on about your company.

Remember, your goal is to hear what the other person has to say. Very quickly, you want to find out more about who they are and what they do. You may not have much time together at the event, so let them do the talking at least 75 percent of the time.

You want to figure out whether this person is someone you plan to follow up with. If you do, make sure you get their business card or exchange contact information, and while you're there, write a little note to remind yourself later of the pertinent facts.

It's easy to keep a note file on your phone, so you have all your notes in one place. Then, within a few days, follow up with key prospects. It's all a waste of time if you don't take that next step.

By the way, not following up is the biggest mistake I see people making in their new business efforts. They attend an event, talk to a few potential prospects, and collect contact information.

Then they get back to the office, get busy on day-to-day work, and don't make the follow-up calls they should be making.

If you're going to attend events, think about it this way: use one-third of your time planning for the event, researching who will be there and who you want to meet; use another third attending the event, and the final third following up.

With a bit of searching, you'll find conferences in your target markets where you can attend and perhaps pursue a speaking opportunity. It will take some practice to get polished at it, but speaking at the right events is a proven way to bring in a steady flow of new business.

One tip about speaking: you're not there to do a straight-out pitch for your services. In your talk, you should be providing information that's useful to your audience and potential clients.

It could be about a new technique or platform that companies like theirs have used successfully, a surprising case study, or an industry overview from a marketing perspective.

If you can find agendas of previous conferences, you'll see the speakers' topics. That will give you an idea of the subject matter they're looking for at this type of gathering. There are many topic angles. Just remember that no one showed up just to hear a commercial for your company.

Be a Guest on a Popular Podcast or Blog

There have never been more content "publishers" than there are today. There are over 1.5 million podcasts[1] and 600 million blogs[2] aimed at various audiences, all looking for material.

Find ones that address your client audiences and see whether you can be a guest. Again, just like speaking at an event, you need something of interest to the audience, not a corporate pitch. Be informative, be newsworthy, be provocative, be funny.

Another Networking Opportunity—Your Suppliers

Your suppliers are likely working with many clients directly. And I know that their clients will ask them for recommendations. Make sure your suppliers know exactly what you do, where you specialize, and that you're always looking for new business.

Word of mouth from a trusted source like a supplier is a powerful way to get new business. You want to do everything you can to promote that.

Most Networking Events are a Waste of Time

You may come across meetings that are billed as networking events. Sometimes they're free. Other times there's an entry fee.

You should avoid most of them. This type of event will be a group of people all trying to pitch whatever they're selling. No one is there to buy—they're all trying to sell. It's unlikely that they'll be your real prospects.

However, there are exceptions. If you're attending an industry event that features potential prospects, and at the end of the day they have a time for networking, then by all means, go. That's assuming you chose the event for a good reason, and it's been a worthwhile day.

This may be a time to talk to someone you noticed but didn't have a chance to meet or to continue a conversation that was cut off earlier.

Writing in the Right Places

If you or someone on your team is a good writer and can make time to write consistently, it can be a powerful marketing tool.

The trick is to find the right outlets for your writing. The first obvious spot is to have a blog on your website. You can also use your blog to show off your employees' expertise—get them to write some of the posts. Publish consistently, promote signing up to the blog and get the message out.

Even better is guest posting—the written equivalent of speaking at an industry event. You want to look for opportunities to provide articles or posts to industry websites, newsletters, and publications.

There's still magic in being published—assuming it's a targeted article, it helps bolster your expertise.

The first places to look are outlets that your current clients read. For example, if you have retail clients, they likely belong to an association with a media outlet or pay attention to industry publications.

All industries have media outlets. It may take some time to find them, but they're out there. Find the editor and get in touch to learn whether they accept submissions.

It's unlikely you'll get paid for it, but you should get your contact information included with the article or guest post. You should also get a link back to your website—it's good for your SEO.

Winning at Awards Shows

Winning awards may not be what gets you the new client, but it helps support your expertise. Ideally, the company running the show will promote the winners, and you should do the same.

If you won an award where business performance was part of the equation, see whether you can get permission from your client to promote the award and the business metrics as a case study through social media, blog posts, or an article.

You want to demonstrate to potential clients that you understand business and that your work helps them grow their sales and communicate with their audiences.

Working Arrangements with Other Companies

Let's say you're a creative agency, but you don't have technical expertise in backend web integration. You could find a company that offers the services you may need for some projects.

Ideally, they may have clients where they could also sell your services.

This worked well for me at Fireworks Creative. At a time when we were a company of 25, we had a working arrangement with a tech company that employed about 300 programmers but with no in-house design or communications capabilities.

Together, we pitched and won some of the most significant web and tech projects that were up for bids, often succeeding in intense competition.

If you can work out the compensation agreements, this type of arrangement can work well. You have to train each other so that you can sell the other firm's services and they can sell yours.

This type of relationship will take some patience to create and manage, but if you do, each company will be much more powerful than they were before.

Tip on making this work for you: if you are the smaller partner in this arrangement (like we were with 25 employees versus their 300), you must find a person in the other company who will be your primary contact.

You need someone to be the champion of this arrangement. Otherwise, it's easy for them to forget about you.

Work with that person to arrange presentations to other members of their team. Make sure they're aware of you, how you best work together, and that their company management has approved your working relationship.

Have a Sales Person on Your Team

This is a tricky one, which is why I have it last. I don't think salespeople are necessary for most creative agencies.

You, the owner, are the best salesperson for your company. You know the company deeply and can answer any questions a prospect might have. In fact, sales should be one of your primary functions.

If you're following the model where you want clients that bring you substantial ongoing business, you are looking for just a few new clients per year.

On the other hand, if you're making videos for hair salons and coffee shops, you need new projects every week, but I doubt there's enough money in it to afford a salesperson.

The other challenge is that salespeople focus on getting their commissions (you can't blame them), and in doing so, they bring you projects you don't want because they don't fit your niche. The salesperson will push for you to accept the work, even though it may be a distraction for you.

However, there are exceptions where salespeople can work. If, for example, you are a programming shop that builds websites, you're not likely working in a narrow vertical, but rather, by a defined deliverable—i.e., websites.

That means you're always looking for new projects, and that's where a salesperson can help.

To get the best value from a salesperson here, you need to work together to ensure they're pursuing the right type of business for your company.

You need strategies for finding clients—perhaps your salesperson is a good speaker, has found a profitable niche answering particular RFPs, or is exceptionally well-connected in specific industries.

I would think hard before pursuing this avenue. Make sure you're comfortable that this type of relationship meets your goals for new clients.

Also, take the time to work out the compensation scenarios. Is the salesperson compensated for every project done by that client forever after? Are there different levels of compensation for various types of projects? There is plenty to consider to make this arrangement work smoothly.

Chapter Takeaways

- Figuring out how to get new clients will take some trial and error. Likely, it will be a combination of efforts.

- Make sure you have your basics in place first: an up-to-date website and social media presence that accurately communicates who you are and what you do. These are musts before adding anything else.
- Look for clients that you want, rather than waiting for random opportunities. Research, interact and then contact these companies and organizations.
- When it comes to networking, go where your potential clients gather. Going to events with your peers is simply a social gathering, which can be fun, but you won't find new business there.
- Consider other options to boost exposure in your client business categories. Writing, speaking, and being a guest contributor are all proven ways to get yourself known.

---

1. Ross Winn, "2020 Podcast Stats & Facts (New Research from Oct 2020)," *PodcastInsights*, October 6, 2020. https://www.podcastinsights.com/podcast-statistics/
2. Kyle Byers, "How Many Blogs Are There? (And 141 Other Blogging Stats.)," *GrowthBadger*, January 2, 2019. https://growthbadger.com/blog-stats/.

23

LEGAL AND INSURANCE

"The devil is in the terms and conditions."

— Aniekee Tochukwu Ezekiel

Signing Non-Disclosure Agreements

At some point, clients will ask you to sign non-disclosure (NDA) or confidentiality agreements. They may be blanket agreements covering all work you do with them or one for a specific project.

An NDA makes you responsible for safeguarding the information that the client provides you.

You shouldn't have a problem with signing one. You won't likely be able to make any changes to the agreement—it's generally a "take it or leave it" proposition, much like the software licenses you agree to without reading them.

Four things to keep in mind:

1. If you have staff, have a meeting to tell them about these agreements and emphasize how important it is to keep

information private. They shouldn't discuss working on these projects over drinks with their friends, family, or anyone.

2. It's worth reminding employees periodically about the importance of confidentiality. If you're given a "super-secret project," call a special staff meeting.

3. If you're working with suppliers on behalf of your clients, they need to know too. You may even have your own NDA that you ask the supplier to sign. You may want further assurances on very confidential matters. For example, is that supplier working for one of your client's competitors? That could be a problem.

4. If the NDA covers a specific project, once that project launches and becomes public, you can generally acknowledge that you worked on it. However, there may still be related background information that isn't public, and you are bound to safeguard it.

Copyright and Ownership of Digital Files

Copyright can be a controversial area. Technically, the copyright of any intellectual property belongs to the creator.

They have the rights to this material and can control how it's used. They may choose to grant specific rights and limit how anyone can reproduce their materials.

There are many established contract types for the use of intellectual property in the world of fine arts. There are also many wealthy copyright lawyers to create and enforce those contracts.

In my businesses, we liked to keep our lives uncomplicated and free of lawyers. Quite simply, anything we created for our clients and that our clients paid for became their property.

Sometimes, with large corporate or government clients, this was explicit in our contracts with them. With most clients, we simply told them that what we created for them, and they paid for, was theirs.

It was essential for us to communicate this to any suppliers we worked with. If we hired a photographer, we made sure they knew that we were giving the rights to their work to the client to use as they saw fit.

For example, we may have hired a photographer to create images for a client's website. As far as we were concerned, the client was free to use those images in their email, social media, or wherever they wanted.

If the photographer couldn't agree to that, we hired someone else. Be sure to review this before hiring a photographer, videographer, or any other content creator. Some may object to it, so don't take it for granted.

These days, with the easy ability to capture and reproduce images, we didn't want the responsibility of policing how a client used the photos.

Our guarantee to the photographer was that the images were only to be used by the client that commissioned them. That meant that we, as the agency, were not allowed to use the images for another client.

We weren't in the business of creating our own stock libraries.

There was also a time when agencies were advised not to hand over digital files to clients. We ignored that. If a client wanted a digital file, we gave it to them, as long as they had paid for it. The fact is, this very rarely came up.

You can choose to handle this however you wish. But I can tell you from experience, having detailed contracts that limit the client's use of materials will complicate your relationship with them. Your goal is to make life easy for your clients.

Getting Liability Insurance

If you start working with larger clients and apply to get on vendor lists, liability insurance will come up. You'll be asked to have liability insurance to cover claims up to millions of dollars. Liability insurance is there to protect you against errors that you or your company were responsible for.

For example, years ago, a friend of mine worked in an agency where they created an ad for a major car company. The ad ran in national magazines. It had a glaring spelling error.

The client had approved the ad. No one noticed the typo before it was published. Rerunning the corrected ad cost tens of thousands of dollars. I hope they had adequate liability insurance.

Liability insurance is expensive. We typically paid $4,000 to $5,000 annually. The first time you're told to get it, you may try to push back, asking whether you REALLY need it.

Like an NDA, if someone requires it, there's no getting around it, and you'll just have to pay to get a policy, which you have to renew every year.

Fortunately, once you do have it, it covers everything you do for all clients up to the insurance amount. We've never had to use it, which is a good thing. Having it was just another cost of doing business.

Avoid Lawsuits—The Only Winners are the Lawyers

My firm once designed a poster for a client that featured a distinctive illustration of a woman floating underwater, dressed in red flowing robes.

Our designer was also an illustrator, and it was his illustration. Everyone, including the client, loved it. The poster was printed and used to promote an event.

Shortly after, we got a letter from a lawyer representing a photographer. Along with the letter was a print of a photograph of a woman floating underwater, dressed in red. It was similar to our illustration.

On behalf of his photographer client, the lawyer was demanding $10,000 in payment for the license to use the photograph as inspiration for our illustration, or they would go to court.

Our designer readily admitted he based his illustration on the photo. However, there were notable differences in the pose and the background, aside from the fact that one was a photo and the other an illustration.

Had we fought it, we might have won. On the other hand, depending on the judge, we may have lost. We didn't think about it for long. We were going to pay. We told our client about it. Graciously, they said they would foot the bill. But even if they hadn't, we would have paid.

That way, we put it behind us. It wouldn't occupy our minds or take up our time. We wouldn't run the risk of losing and then paying fees to our lawyer, their lawyer, plus the $10,000.

Protect Yourself from Lawsuits as Much as Possible

I'm assuming you're behaving ethically in all of your business dealings. You're not out there stealing, cheating, trying to rip off others.

You deliver on your projects as outlined in your estimates. You have consulted with a lawyer on any contracts you've signed. You have liability insurance that will pay for expensive mistakes.

However, if despite all of this, someone wants to sue you, look for other ways to settle. You could simply pay the demand or look for a mediated settlement to keep it out of the courts. Both options will likely be less expensive and faster to resolve.

I'm sure there is someone out there in the creative agency business who's happy with the outcome after going to court, but I have yet to meet them.

Don't "Lawyer Up"

For a very short time, my company had a client we obviously shouldn't have taken on. He came to us through an introduction and wanted a website and marketing materials for his new company.

From the beginning, he seemed to know everything better than anyone else. No matter what we proposed and presented, it was never quite what he had in mind.

We were partway through the project, and it was time for him to pay an interim bill of about $6,000, as outlined in the estimate. (Yes, we should have demanded a deposit before starting!)

He refused to pay, saying he was still not satisfied with work to date and he would pay the full amount of the invoice upon completion. He wanted us to proceed with the project assuming it would somehow turn out the way he had envisioned.

We had three choices:

1. We could proceed as he suggested.
2. We could get a lawyer to send him a demand letter for the outstanding amount.
3. We could walk away from the project and write off $6,000 of work.

We chose option three. We doubted we would ever get paid for the whole project, given that he hadn't paid us anything. We didn't want to pay for dueling lawyers. We just wanted to move on and put this behind us.

Disagreements in our business are usually about money. That's why it's essential to protect yourself by getting deposits and progress payments as you work through the project. Don't allow yourself to be in a situation where someone owes you a considerable amount but refuses to pay.

The non-payment of the interim bill was our warning and protected us from losing even more. This client was an extraordinary case. There haven't been any others, and during my time, we never went to court against a client.

Chapter Takeaways

- Take care of legal requirements and abide by them.
- Stay out of court.
- Keep your life simple. You've got enough to think about.

AFTERWORD

When All is Said and Done...

"And in the end, the love you take is equal to the love you make."

— Paul McCartney

There are many types of creative agencies and many ways to run an agency. What I've written about here worked for me. If you start an agency, you'll find your own way. I hope that you can use some of my experience to help you grow and flourish. Here are a few of my closing thoughts.

Relationships Are Everything

The creative agency business is all about relationships. You are not a solo writer hammering out novels in a garret or a painter alone in a cold studio.

You'll work with clients, partners, employees, freelancers, and suppliers. Of this list, the most important are clients and partners. The others will come and go. I was lucky to form strong relationships with many clients (not all) and my partners.

It's easier than ever to work remotely, to connect on screens. And while this was a necessity during the pandemic, once that's over, I think the value of being face-to-face with key people will be greater than ever.

Think about the conversations that inevitably come up in remote relationships.

"Hey, we should get together. When are you coming out here?"

"I'll be in L.A. next month. Let's set up a time to meet."

"Yeah, let's grab dinner."

The urge to be together, to connect in person, is strong. We are social animals. Use it in your business to your advantage.

Partnerships Helped Me Build

For me, having a business partner was natural. It's what I learned as an ad agency copywriter. I was paired with an art director, and we worked together, bouncing ideas off each other and finally coming up with ads and other marketing materials.

When I decided to grow from being a solo freelance copywriter, I instinctively looked for a graphic design partner.

I could have just found an employee, but I wanted someone as committed to the company as I was. I also wanted someone who had experience running their own business and had existing clients to bring to the new enterprise.

You may see it differently. If your instinct is to work alone, say as a programmer, you may be more inclined to either hire full-time or by the project but not bring on a partner. You have to know yourself to decide how you want to structure your company at the top of the pyramid.

However, if you want to continue being a practitioner (writer, designer, programmer, photographer), remember, you're also running the company and keeping an eye on the finances. You'll need strong people right alongside you to take care of those aspects.

Pay Attention to Finances

We're creators, not accountants. We'd rather talk about coming up with the next great idea than reviewing financial reports. However, this is a business, not a hobby, and money is essential to keep it going and growing.

You may have to force yourself to pay attention to the numbers, learn what they mean, and act based on what you've learned. If you're not the one to do it, you need a partner or business advisor to focus on that aspect.

There's no getting around it. You have to understand your numbers and adjust accordingly.

Evolving with the Times

As the saying goes, the only constant is change. In marketing and related media, change has been dramatic since the mid-1990s.

Where once most marketing communications centered around television, radio, newspapers, magazines, and direct mail, today it's Internet-based with dozens of technologies riding on the digital backbone. That gives us websites, email, blogs, podcasts, video, social media, and various streaming services.

For creators forming agencies, it means making decisions on which technologies and platforms to integrate into the company's offering.

It's easiest if the new technology is a relatively simple iteration of an existing one that you already provide. For example, as a filmmaker, you could transition into TikTok, along the way learning what would make that platform useful for your clients.

The critical point is to keep up in a way that makes sense for your agency and your clients. You don't want to be everything to everyone, but you do want to stay relevant.

How Do Agencies Transition or How Do You Exit?

Let's look at two typical scenarios.

In scenario one, let's say that you and your partners want to sell the agency for whatever reason. You want someone to buy the company so that you're paid out and can transition out of the business.

Let's assume that no one has approached you with an offer, so you would have to take the initiative and look for a buyer. Before you start, realize this process could take a few years, so plan accordingly.

Let's first look at who the possible buyers might be:

- A bigger agency is looking to expand. They might be interested in your agency because of your capabilities in a specific physical location. For example, they want an L.A. office that offers the services that you provide and think it's easier to buy your L.A. agency than to build their own from the ground up.
- An agency or perhaps a tech company that wants to add your particular expertise to their existing offering. This

is a likely possibility for agencies with narrowly defined specialties. Your agency might be a social media agency, an email marketing provider, an influencer marketing company, or a company with a particular vertical expertise, such as the medical field. A larger company might want to add that expertise to their client offering and have decided it's easier to buy than build.

- Another company that is similar to yours and wants to accelerate growth through acquisition. They're hoping that 1+1=3, where the sum of the two agencies would give them a more prominent profile and make them eligible for larger accounts.
- Some of your employees might find the funding to buy the business.

Before you go to market, you need to review a few critical aspects of your business to make yourself as attractive as possible.

The first is your finances. You should be profitable, preferably, very profitable over and above what you pay yourself. Any potential buyer wants to know that you've built a successful business. You'll likely work with a financial consultant to tidy up any loose ends in your books.

Second, you'll want to demonstrate that you have long-term relationships with substantial clients.

Although clients are free to leave at any time, the fact that you have long client relationships shows that your company can satisfy their requirements over many years and would likely do the same for similar clients in the future.

If you have the type of agency where you depend on a steady flow of smaller clients, you'll need to demonstrate that you have a proven sales process that brings in constant streams of business.

Third, you'll want to show that your company works with robust internal processes and is not dependent on the presence of current management.

In other words, someone else could step in and follow those processes and get a successful, profitable outcome.

It's difficult if the agency is just about you, because what happens when you're gone? This is a problem with some agencies built around a star name, such as a high-profile creative director. Potential buyers will doubt the value of the agency without the star.

This also factors into relationships with clients. Will clients stay if the star leaves? Typically, if a buyer is interested in the agency, even with a star running it, they will look for the transition to take place over years.

This lets them wean clients off the relationship with any given person and get them working with the new group.

Also, the payout will depend on the performance of the agency over that time. This type of payout, over a period of years where the amount is dependent on performance, is called an "earn-out."

Let's look at the option of a group of employees buying the agency. These would be senior employees who can find the funds (mortgage the house) to buy the agency. The terms of sale will likely be a payout over a few years.

Realistically, this can only happen if you have a level of senior employees who can envision themselves as owners and have the financial resources to make the deal work.

Once your agency is prepped for sale, you may want to find a consultant who can help you market your business and find potential buyers.

You can find consultants by asking your accountant who should know some of them. After all, accountants are deeply involved in the buying and selling of companies. If your accountant can't help, do a search.

Now, let's look at scenario two. In this case, you are a partner in the agency and would like to leave the company to retire or do something else. Here is where your partnership agreement comes into play. It should address how the company deals with this type of transition.

Typically, it involves having the company evaluated, which will be related to its billing and profitability over several years. Based on that, you come to an agreement with the other partners and get paid out.

You'll likely be paid over several years. In my case, my payout was paid every two weeks, like a salary, over four years.

In both scenarios, you'll want to work with your accountant to find the most tax-efficient way to get paid. Events such as selling or getting paid out of your company will have an impact on your taxes. Plan ahead.

The Real Story About What Happens to Many Creative Agencies

Often, after decades in business, many small agencies simply fade away with no big payout for anyone. That's because they haven't planned for a better exit.

Typically, these agencies haven't changed with the times, haven't specialized, don't have specific systems in place, and most of their clients are based on personal relationships with the owner.

These agencies may have provided an excellent living for the owner and competitive salaries for employees, but there's no residual value in the company. There's nothing that someone else couldn't easily replicate, and in all likelihood, there's little that will remain when the owner leaves.

Once you've established your agency, it's worth thinking about how you will eventually exit. You want to build a company that will be of value to someone else. If not, at some point, you will close that door for the last time and call it a day.

Last Words—Take the First Step

If you've thought about starting an agency more than once, just do it. Do a brain dump about what you have in mind for the agency, think about it some more, organize your thoughts into a cohesive plan, and get on with it.

Once you start the ball rolling, good things will happen, things you can't even imagine now.

It's an interesting phenomenon. Tell people about your new venture. They'll want to hear about it. People like stories about start-ups, about new businesses. They will cheer you on and try to help you. They'll make suggestions (some of which might be useful) and introduce you to others as their entrepreneur friend.

Assuming you bring someone on as a partner or employee, you now have a bigger story to tell your existing clients.

You'll also want to update your website and social media. Get the word out. With more capabilities, you'll be in line for more significant projects.

And now the ball has started rolling down the hill. Good luck!

ACKNOWLEDGMENTS

A big thank you to those who helped me along the way. I know I've missed some people, so apologies in advance.

Nancy Armstrong, Brian Baker, Tony Begbie, Ronald Brisebois, Simon Burn, Roger Carstairs, Steve Comrie, Patrick Connor, John Ecker, Paul Fiala, Lionel Gadoury, Arthur Gelgoot, Ben Hagon, Cate Jevons, Stan Kates, Jacqueline Kroft, Barry McCabe, Dan Natale, Wendy Novachko, Catherine Parry, Blair Peberdy, Ian Roberts, Margaret Robertson, Aldous Silva, Kevin Sterling, Jeff Tapping, Marina Tomasone, Sharry Wilson

.